The ★★★★ GYMNASTICS ALMANAC

By Luan Peszek

ROXBURY PARK

LOWELL HOUSE JUVENILE

LOS ANGELES

NTC/Contemporary Publishing Group

Photos provided by AllSport, USA
Cover photo © AllSport, USA/Tony Duffy. All rights reserved.

Published by Lowell House
A division of NTC/Contemporary Publishing Group, Inc.
4255 West Touhy Avenue, Lincolnwood (Chicago), Illinois 60646-1975 U.S.A.

Lowell House books can be purchased at special discounts when ordered in bulk for
premiums and special sales. Contact Department CS at the following address:
NTC/Contemporary Publishing Group
4255 W. Touhy Avenue
Lincolnwood, IL 60646-1975
1-800-323-4900

ISBN:1-56565-966-X

Library of Congress Catalog Card Number: 98-067405

Roxbury Park is a division of NTC/Contemporary Publishing Group, Inc.

Managing Director and Publisher: Jack Artenstein
Editor in Chief, Roxbury Park Books: Michael Artenstein
Director of Publishing Services: Rena Copperman
Managing Editor: Lindsey Hay

Printed and bound in the United States of America
10 9 8 7 6 5 4 3 2 1

Thanks to my wonderful husband, Ed, and two daughters, Samantha and Jessica. Also thanks to my supportive parents, who drove me to gymnastics practice my entire life and encouraged my love for gymnastics.

—LP

CONTENTS

CHAPTER 1

GETTING STARTED

Would you like to learn how to roll, flip, twist, climb, swing, and fly? These are the things you will get to do at gymnastics class. Do you have a lot of energy and like to be busy all the time? Then gymnastics may be just the sport for you!

When people think of gymnastics, they often think of the Olympians they have seen on television dozens of times. Actually, what people see on television is just the elite level of the sport. These gymnasts are the best in the country and sometimes the best in the world. When the elite gymnasts perform their routines, gymnastics looks very easy, but that's what they've been trained to do—make something difficult look effortless and graceful.

Have you thought of trying the sport of gymnastics? Maybe you're not sure you're "gymnast material." Well, anyone can participate in the sport of gymnastics. Not everyone can be the next Olga, Nadia, Mary Lou, or member of the Magnificent Seven team, but you *can* have fun and learn a number of skills in the process. And who knows—you may turn out to be the next superstar in the sport!

Gymnastics develops many positive attributes including strength, flexibility, agility, coordination, speed, balance, and rhythm. Gymnastics also teaches you how to set goals and learn self-confidence, self-respect,

What it Takes

Gymnastics participation demands concentration. Without concentration, you may fall and get hurt. Many good gymnasts are also good students. Why? Because they've mastered concentration, focus, and goal-setting. They also have great time-management skills. They realize they must do homework first in order to go to gymnastics practice. They have their priorities in order!

expressiveness, determination, time management, and courage.

Whether you're dreaming of becoming the next Shannon Miller or you just want to learn a few skills so you can become a better cheerleader or soccer player, gymnastics is a great sport for you.

Did you know that what you learn in gymnastics can help you in other sports? Many athletes start out in the sport of gymnastics and then move to another sport when they are a little older. Gymnastics is a great basic foundation for all kids because it teaches speed, agility, coordination, flexibility, confidence, and strength—all the attributes that are necessary for success in other sports as well.

Gymnastics is one of the only sports in which a small child can participate. Have you ever seen a two-year-old child playing tennis? Have you ever seen a five-year-old child playing football? Probably not. That's because these sports require skills such as running, jumping, and hand-eye coordination—things that are developed in gymnastics!

Many kids worry that they will be too tall to participate in gymnastics, but anyone can participate in gymnastics and learn many skills. And if you decide to move on to another sport, you'll have the basics under your belt. You may even be one step ahead of your teammates.

If you've decided you want to give gymnastics a try, you must first find a gymnastics school or program to join. Look in the yellow pages of the phone book under GYMNASTICS to locate a facility in your area. You may also want to look under the headings DANCE, FITNESS, or HEALTH CLUBS. There are many local recreational gymnastics programs that may be excellent but not affiliated with any of the major gymnastics organizations. Ask around in your community and perhaps you'll learn about a quality gymnastics program in your own neighborhood.

You can also call USA Gymnastics at 1-800-345-4719 and they can help you locate a gym near you. USA Gymnastics also has a website (www.usa-gymnastics.org), which has a club search section to help you find a gymnastics program in your area.

Once you find a gym in your area, the next step is to visit the facility and see what it has to offer.

Gymnastics clubs offer many types of programs. Some examples include a class for toddlers and their parents. This class involves more body-movement-type activities than gymnastics skills. One- to three-year-old children may crawl through tunnels, slide down slides, bounce balls, swing on bars, and learn to run and roll during a forty-five-minute class. There may be themes to each class such as colors, numbers, or shapes, and many props are used, including balls, balloons, bean bags, scooters, and ropes. Most "Mommy and Me" classes use music, and their basic goal is to teach coordination and basic motor skills.

Preschool classes introduce basic body positions such as the tuck, pike, straddle, and layout. Like the "Mommy and Me" class, props such as balls, balloons, bean bags, scooters, and ropes are utilized. This class also introduces jumping, skipping, and running.

Beginner classes for ages five and up go over the basics of the sport. You must take a beginner class and learn the basics before you can move up.

Intermediate and advanced classes build on what you've learned so far and may last from one hour to one hour and a half. For example, if you haven't mastered a cartwheel, then you can't learn a side aerial, which is a cartwheel with no hands.

When is the right age to start gymnastics?

There is no right age. Some start at age two while others start at twelve. It's never too late to learn!

According to the *USA Gymnastics Safety Handbook,* here are some student-to-teacher ratio suggestions for recreational gymnastics classes:

AGE OF STUDENT	SKILLS	EQUIPMENT	RATIO
			(STUDENT TO TEACHER)
5 years	basic tumbling	basic mats	6 to 1
10 years	basic skills	various events	8–10 to 1
16 years	basic skills	various events	8–15 to 1

These are only examples! Each teaching situation will dictate the appropriate range of student-to-teacher ratios.

If you dream of making the gymnastics team program, then you will need to devote more time to the sport and master the basics. Coaches typically select gymnasts for the team program from as early as age five (preteam), all the way up to high school age.

Once you're on a team program, the time commitment involved is more than the class program. For example, a Level 4 gymnast may train four to seven hours per week and a Level 9 gymnast may train fourteen to seventeen hours per week.

Some gyms offer programs like cheerleading class, tumbling class, or trampoline class.

Here are some questions to consider when visiting a gym. Some may apply to you and others may not!

- **Is the gym clean and do the coaches look and act professional?**
- **Does the gym have updated and age-appropriate equipment?**
- **Does all the equipment have mats underneath?**
- **What do the gymnasts and parents say about the program?**
- **Does the gym have a competitive team?**
- **Do the coaches seem knowledgeable and friendly?**
- **Are the gym's class times and location convenient for you and your parents?**
- **Does the gym have the program you're interested in trying?**
- **Does it look like a place you'd like to hang out?**
- **Are the kids in the classes having fun?**
- **Does the cost fit into your family budget?**
- **What are you supposed to wear to class?**
- **How long does the class last?**
- **Does the gym close for holidays?**

It's always a good idea to observe a class at the facility before you sign up. Some clubs may even let you take a trial class to see if you like it before you sign up for a six- or eight-week session, which is usually what is offered.

You'll also want to find out how much the classes are and what other costs are involved. It's hard to predict how much classes cost because it depends on what part of the country you live in and what type of facility you want to try. Some gymnastics clubs require a one-time or yearly registration fee. Some clubs charge for lessons by the month and others charge by the session, which may last six, eight or twelve weeks.

The good thing about gymnastics lessons is that there is no major equipment purchase necessary. Figure skaters have to buy skates, softball players need a mitt, soccer players need shin pads and a ball, golfers need golf clubs, and water-skiers need skis, but gymnasts use the equipment provided by the facility!

Keep in mind that most gymnastics facilities will ask that the girls wear a leotard or tight-fitting shorts and shirt and no shoes. Do not wear loose-fitting shorts because they could get wrapped around the bars. Shirts should be tucked in to prevent them from blocking your vision when you roll or hang upside down. Zippers, buttons, and snaps should be avoided because they may scratch or hurt you or your teacher. If you have long hair, it must be kept out of your face and eyes. Also, do not wear jewelry because it could also get caught on a piece of equipment or harm the coach. Be careful of slippery socks—you may want to go barefoot to be safe!

You might want to ask where your parents can sit. Most gyms have an observation area for the students' parents and siblings. You can find your family members after class in this area.

Well, you're ready to begin your gymnastics class. Have fun and listen to the coach. You'll be flipping in no time!

Did you know . . .

USA Gymnastics has more than 70,000 registered competitive gymnasts in the United States, and girls outnumber boys five to one? This number doesn't even include all the other kids in the country who are taking gymnastics classes.

CHAPTER 2

SAFETY FIRST

Gymnastics, like any sport you try, can be dangerous. According to the *USA Gymnastics Safety Manual,* your philosophy in the sport of gymnastics should be "Safety first, second, and always."

Although most gymnastics clubs try to eliminate all potential dangers in the gym, injuries still may occur. The most common gymnastics injuries involve the lower leg and lower arm.

It's important to keep in mind that what you see the gymnasts do on television may look easy, but it has taken years and years of training for them to excel. It didn't just happen overnight. After you take a couple of gymnastics classes, you'll probably find that it's anything but easy. Just like a baby learns to walk before she can run, a gymnast must first learn to roll before she can flip.

Don't walk into the gym, throw your body into the air, and hope to land safely. You must take things one step at a time, listen to your instructor, and work up to the big skills.

Also, be careful about coming home after your first day at gymnastics class and trying to show your mom the back walkover that your coach was helping you with. Remember, you need mats, instruction, and spotting on new skills that you're just learning. If you want to practice something at home, work on your splits, sit-ups, push-ups, jump rope, and other conditioning drills to make you more flexible and strong. These are safe and good for your body.

The Warm-Up

Most gymnastics classes start out with a warm-up activity, which lasts five to ten minutes to get your body loose and ready for physical activity.

Try not to be late to gymnastics class, because your body needs to get warmed up before you jump right into a gymnastics activity.

Warm-up activities can take many forms, from running through an obstacle course to dancing to skipping rope. The exercise should be fairly simple but cause you to breathe hard!

Flexibility is a key to gymnastics, so many warm-ups may begin with jogging, jumping, hopping, or skipping-type activities, followed by stretching to gain flexibility.

Working on splits (right side, left side, and middle) is also very common in a gymnastics warm-up. Advanced gymnasts work on splits by putting their heel up on an elevated mat (typically about four inches high) and oversplitting. There are many types of stretches used to help you with flexibility. Your instructor will be able to

Dominique Moceanu on beam at the 1996 Olympic Games

Safety first!

There are many rules you should always keep in mind while at gymnastics class, and your instructor will probably go over them before your first class. Here are a few rules to keep in mind:

• Always make sure your instructor is present before you begin your gymnastics class.

• There should only be one person on the equipment at a time unless your instructor gives you specific directions otherwise. (For example, if you are trying pull-ups on the uneven bars, then the instructor may allow two gymnasts on the bars at one time, with a gymnast on either end of the bar.)

• You should look both ways before you cross in front of another class. Otherwise, you may be run over by a gymnast vaulting or tumbling or dismounting from the beam!

show you some drills for gaining flexibility. The most important thing to remember with flexibility exercises is not to bounce but rather to hold the stretch. Children should hold a stretch for at least twenty seconds, and adults should hold a stretch for at least forty seconds to get results.

Back flexibility is also very important in the sport of gymnastics. Beginning classes will have you bridge up to a back bend from the floor and hold the position. As you advance you will learn to start from a standing position and arch back to a back bend.

Gymnastics classes should conclude with a cool-down activity such as light stretching and simple movements to help your body make the transition from the vigorous training activity to a normal state.

Progressions

Progressions are the key to learning gymnastics safely and efficiently. A progression takes you through the individual steps necessary to accomplish a skill. For example, if you were learning a back handspring, your coach may first have you jump backward onto a big fluffy mat, landing on your back with your arms by your ears in a tight body position. Why? This would give you the feeling of going backward and it would ensure that you are sitting and jumping in the proper position. The coach would help you learn the proper technique for this first progression. Once you've mastered it, the coach may have you do the back handspring over a large octagonal mat. Why? Because you'll get the feeling of doing the trick, but if you don't make it, you'll land on the soft mat and you won't hurt yourself. Do you get the idea of progressions?

If your instructor tells you to try your back handspring on the floor by yourself and you've never done one before, you may want to find a new gymnastics program, because safety is certainly not a priority for this gym!

Here's another example of a progression—using the balance beam. Before you learn a cartwheel on the high beam, you must master the skill on the floor. Then you may try the cartwheel on the floor beam. Next you may try the skill on the medium-size beam with a beam pad. Then you'll remove

A warm-up:

- Engorges the major muscle groups with blood (heats up the body temperature).

- Elevates the heart rate.

- Takes the muscles and joints through an appropriate range of motion.

17

the beam pad, and finally you'll perform the cartwheel on the high beam.

A gymnast will learn a handstand on the floor and master this element before trying to put it up on the beam, bars, or vault. However, once a handstand is mastered on floor exercise, a gymnast has the basics necessary for learning a handspring vault, cast handstand on bars, and English handstand on beam. It is important to learn tumbling skills in an orderly and progressive manner—paying attention to the basics is crucial. Every skill you learn in tumbling will help you learn more

A gymnast must master the handstand on the floor before trying it on the beam.

difficult skills, both in tumbling and in other events. Don't take shortcuts just to learn a skill for its own sake; take the time and extra effort to learn the skill correctly. This will help you in the long run. Don't skimp on the basics. Learn the basics with precision, amplitude, and grace and you'll go far.

Training aids are also popular in teaching gymnastics. A training aid is something you can use to learn a particular skill. For example, an instructor teaching handstands will have you kick up to the handstand against a mat that is leaning against the wall, which holds you in place. That way students can practice their handstands against the wall on their own while the instructor moves around the room, helping different students.

Here's another example of a training aid. On vault, the instructor may pile up the mats on the opposite side of the vaulting board. The instructor then teaches you how to do a handspring and land flat on your back on the mats. The instructor is using the mats as a training aid to help you learn the first part of the skill. Once you've got the first part of the skill, the instructor may have you jump off the horse and try to stick. Why? Because the instructor is teaching you proper landing drills.

There are other ways that instructors teach gymnastics. The instructor may spot you, which means manually assist you to encourage the proper body position, facilitate the correct movement sequence, and protect you. The instructor may put you in a hand belt or an overhead belt. The hand belt

What to do if you twist your ankle at gymnastics class

The RICE Method

Rest the area to avoid further damage and foster healing.

Ice the area to reduce swelling and pain.

Compress the area by securing an ice bag in place with an elastic wrap.

Elevate the injury above heart level to keep the blood from pooling in the area.

If swelling, pain, or loss of function is evident after applying RICE, you should get it checked out by a medical professional.

requires two experienced instructors to use a spotting belt with ropes. It's somewhat inefficient with larger groups since it requires two experienced spotters and each athlete must wear a belt. The overhead belt only requires one spotter but is still not very efficient since the students have to get in and out of the belt.

Another form of spotting is the hands-off, or safety spotting. This is when the coach positions himself in an area where the gymnast might encounter a problem. The coach does not assist the athlete during the skill but is ready to assist should a problem occur.

Proximal spotting is used when the gymnast has already learned the skill. This is when the coach is not in a position to physically spot the gymnast but remains close enough to provide verbal cues, reinforcements, and individualized instruction to the gymnast.

Beginning in August of 1998, gymnastics may get just a little safer. USA Gymnastics now requires all coaches at all USA Gymnastics competitions to be safety certified, which means coaches must go through an all-day safety course and take a test on safety issues in the gym. Just like individuals must pass a driver's test in order to get a driver's license, coaches must now pass this safety test in order to get a "coaching license." This will make the sport safer for you!

Athlete Wellness

Athlete wellness is also a part of gymnastics and any other sport in which you participate. Physical, psychological, and nutritional readiness are all key components to a safe and healthy experience in the sport. USA Gymnastics has undertaken an Athlete Wellness Program, and its goal is to ensure it is doing everything possible to educate and inform its members on ways to encourage lifelong wellness for its athletes.

Prior to starting a gymnastics class, you should be examined by a physician to make sure you're healthy and able to participate in

gymnastics. Some clubs even require you to have a written doctor's note that indicates you've been checked out. You should also come to the gym mentally prepared with a positive outlook.

You should fuel your body with proper nutrition to ensure you'll have energy to participate in class. Just like a car needs gas and oil in order to run, your body needs food and water. Remember to feed your body healthy foods and lots of water to keep it running smoothly. Too many chips, candy bars, and donuts—and not enough meats, fruits, vegetables, and other healthy foods—may cause your body to need a tune-up.

Gymnastics is a physically demanding sport, and you need to prepare your body for it. It's your responsibility to take care of your body—especially when you're asking so much of it.

CHAPTER 3

A GYMNASTICS HISTORY LESSON

Gymnastics has been in existence for more than two thousand years. According to ancient writings and artwork from the period, gymnastics began around 2600 B.C. in Greece and Egypt, where individuals participated in some form of tumbling and acrobatic movements. Gymnastics was not always a fun activity limited to a gymnasium, though; rather, it was once used for military training in ancient Greece in order to ensure that the men were in shape. In fact, a wooden horse was used to practice mounting and dismounting and evolved into what we now know as the pommel horse.

The term *gymnastics* is derived from the Greek word *gymnos,* which means "naked." The term was coined because young men would practice strenuous exercises in the nude—in public!

Gymnastics as an organized competitive sport began to develop just a little more than one hundred years ago. What we think of as modern gymnastics began in Europe in the nineteenth century. Countries such as Switzerland, Sweden, Denmark, Germany, and Czechoslovakia, to name a few, were the first to develop the sport of gymnastics.

In fact, the sport of gymnastics has taken many forms over the past hundred years. What we now know as women's artistic gymnastics (vault, uneven parallel bars, balance beam, and floor exercise) and men's artistic gymnastics (floor exercise, pommel horse, still rings, vault, parallel bars, and horizontal bar) used to include such events as Indian club swinging, tumbling, rope climbing, swimming, and even track-and-field events, all under the umbrella of gymnastics. Up until 1952, women even competed in the same events as men!

Frederich Jahn from Germany is generally considered the father of modern gymnastics. He invented the horizontal bar, still rings, and parallel bars. He was also responsible for developing gymnastics as part of the educational system throughout Europe.

Jahn had a great impact on American gymnastics as well, since Europeans were the first to introduce the sport to the United States. During the 1800s, group and individual exhibitions were conducted by various schools, athletic clubs, and ethnic organizations such as the Turnvereins and Sokols. Although gymnastics was slow to catch on in schools, the sport flourished in private clubs. It was introduced to the United States' school system by such individuals as Carl Beck, Charles Follen, and Francis Lieber. In the 1800s gymnastics was developed in American universities, and Princeton University was the first to have a full-scale gymnasium on its campus.

Gymnastics has certainly grown since the 1800s. In fact, gymnastics is now part of an entire "Olympic family" of organizations.

The Olympic Family

The Olympic family is made up of several organizations, including the International Olympic Committee, the International Gymnastics Federation, the United States Olympic Committee, and USA Gymnastics.

The International Olympic Committee (IOC) governs all Olympic sports all over the world. The IOC was created in 1894 and was entrusted with the control and development of the modern Olympic

Games. If there is a question concerning the Olympic Games, the IOC is the final authority on the subject.

The International Gymnastics Federation, known as the FIG, was formed in 1881 as the Bureau of the European Gymnastics Federation and directs the sport of gymnastics in the world. The FIG establishes the rules on eligibility that each country with a national gymnastics federation must follow. The United States has four representatives who are members of the FIG: Jackie Fie, Jay Ashmore, Andrea Schmid-Shapiro, and George Beckstead.

*Konrad Schwarzemann at the 1936
Olympic Games in Berlin*

James E. Sullivan, founder of the Amateur Athletic Union, began the United States Olympic Committee (USOC) along with a few other people. A. G. Spalding, a publisher and sporting goods manufacturer, became the first elected president of the committee in 1900.

The United States Olympic Committee is comprised of member organizations such as USA Gymnastics, and is the moving force of support for sports in the United States. The USOC is recognized by the IOC and is responsible for underwriting the expenses for the U.S. teams in the Olympics and Pan American Games. The USOC is the guardian of the Olympic movement in America. The USOC also supports the bid of American cities to host winter and summer Olympic Games or Pan American Games. The USOC visits cities during site surveys and selects one city to endorse as "the U.S. City." This city then enters a bid and competes against other cities in the world to host major events.

The USOC holds a "processing" for athletes prior to each Olympic Games. During processing, the Olympians are outfitted in shirts, shorts, jackets, sweatshirts, watches, shoes, pants, hats, and other items that are contributed by sponsors of the USOC to help the athletes in their quest for Olympic gold.

In 1883, the United States' Amateur Athletic Union acted as the national governing body of gymnastics. In 1970, the United States Gymnastics Federation, now known as USA Gymnastics, became the national governing body and remains so today.

USA Gymnastics, headquartered in Indianapolis, Indiana, gets its designation from the IOC and the FIG. USA Gymnastics is responsible for guiding the growth of gymnastics in the United States. In fact, the mission of USA Gymnastics is to encourage participation and the pursuit of excellence in all aspects of gymnastics. USA Gymnastics sets the rules and policies that govern gymnastics in this country. The non-profit organization is also responsible for the selection and training of the USA National Teams and selecting teams for the World Championships and Olympic Games. These are just a few of the many responsibilities of USA Gymnastics. Departments include men's, women's, rhythmic, and general gymnastics; membership; events;

safety and education; marketing; television and sponsorships; public relations; publications; merchandise; and accounting. Gymnastics involves a lot more than just the sport itself!

USA Gymnastics has many constituent organizations represented on its board. These organizations include:

- Amateur Athletic Union
- American Sokol Organization
- American Turners
- College Gymnastics Association
- Jewish Community Centers
- National Association of Collegiate Gymnastics Coaches/Women
- National Association for Girls and Women in Sports
- National Association of Women's Gymnastics Judges
- National Collegiate Athletic Association
- National Federation of State High School Associations
- National Gymnastics Judges Association
- National High School Gymnastics Coaches Association
- Special Olympics, Inc.
- U.S. Association of Independent Gymnastics Clubs
- U.S. Competitive Sports Aerobics Federation
- U.S. Elite Coaches Association for Men
- U.S. Elite Coaches Association for Women
- U.S. Men's Gymnastics Coaches Association
- U.S. Rhythmic Coaches Association
- U.S. Sports Acrobatics Federation
- USA Trampoline & Tumbling Association
- Young Men's Christian Association of the USA

These constituent organizations have played key roles in the development and growth of the sport of gymnastics, especially at the grassroots level.

In the 1960s, the United States had roughly 7,000 registered competitive athletes in gymnastics, with only a handful of national-

and international-level competitions held throughout the year. In 1998, the United States has approximately 70,000 registered competitive athletes in the sport and an additional 13,000 professional members including coaches, judges, club owners, and administrators. Plus, there are about 3,000 competitions and events held annually. The sport is growing by leaps and bounds!

The Olympics and World Championships

The 1896 Olympics in Athens, Greece, was the first major gymnastics competition, and Germany swept the sport's events. Male gymnasts from five countries competed in events that included horizontal bar, parallel bars, pommel horse, rings, and vault. Although the United States' men's program had developed enough to form a team, the Americans did not compete because of the time and money involved in going to the Games in Greece. At that time, gymnastics was developing in athletic clubs, YMCAs, Sokols, and Turner societies across the United States.

Istvan Pelle wins gold on the pommel horse and floor exercise at the 1932 Olympic Games.

In 1903, male gymnasts from Belgium, France, Luxembourg, and the Netherlands competed in the first World Championships in Antwerp, Belgium.

During the 1904 Olympic Games in St. Louis, Missouri, the first in which an American gymnast earned a medal, the events contested included the team event, parallel bars, vault, rope climb, still rings, pommel horse, horizontal bar, and Indian clubs. The U.S. gymnasts earned twenty-one medals during the Games, which were held as part of the World's Fair. Gymnasts from Austria, Germany, and Switzerland won individual all-around medals.

For many years, there were no set events or format for the competition. Depending on the preferences of the host country of the Olympic Games, the gymnastics apparatus and events could change. For example, at the 1922 World Gymnastics Championships in Antwerp, Belgium, officials added swimming and track-and-field events to the competition to attract a bigger audience. (Imagine how the

George Gulack at the 1932 Olympic Games

Russians would have reacted at the 1996 Olympic Games in Atlanta if the organizing committee had said, "Oh, by the way, we're going to compete in high jump today as well as on vault, uneven bars, balance beam, and floor exercise events"!) Officials quickly decided that swimming shouldn't be included, but track-and-field events remained a part of the World Championships until 1954.

Americans didn't earn another medal in gymnastics until the 1924 Olympic Games, when Frank Kriz won a gold medal on vault, a traditional gymnastics event.

Women's gymnastics entered the picture in 1928 at the Olympic Games in Amsterdam in the Netherlands. The U.S. women did not compete as a team at this debut event (they didn't have one yet) but entered a team at the 1936 Olympic Games for the first time.

At the 1930 World Championships in Luxembourg, the competition for men included pole vault, broad jump, shot put, rope climb, and a 100-meter sprint in addition to their already demanding gymnastics events.

At the 1932 Olympic Games in Los Angeles, the U.S. Men's Team won the silver medal and fifteen individual medals. At this competition, several specialty events were added, including rope climbing, Indian club swinging, and tumbling. The Americans excelled in these events, which helped them earn medals. However, rope climbing, tumbling, and Indian club swinging were not continued in later years. No women's competition was contested at these Games.

At their first Olympic Games in 1936 in Berlin, Germany, the U.S. women finished fifth in the team event. The events included compulsory and optional routines on uneven parallel bars, balance beam, and vault, and two optional team drills (one freehand and the other with hand apparatus).

No Olympics were held in 1940 or 1944 because of World War II.

The U.S. Women first medaled at the 1948 Olympic Games, earning the team bronze medal. Members of the team included: Laddie Bakanic,

Marion Barone, Dorothy Dalton, Meta Elste, Consetta Lenz, Helen Schifano, Clara Schroth, and Anita Simonis. Individual events for women, including vault, uneven bars, balance beam, and floor exercise were added in 1952, which is also the first Olympics in which women's gymnastics was recognized as a different sport from men's gymnastics.

The Soviet Union Women's Team, who entered for the first time in 1952, won the team title at every Olympics from 1952–1980. They boycotted the Games in 1984 but came back in 1988 to win another title. At the 1992 Olympics in Barcelona, Spain, the Soviet Union was undergoing major change and was called the Unified Team. The Unified Team won yet another team title.

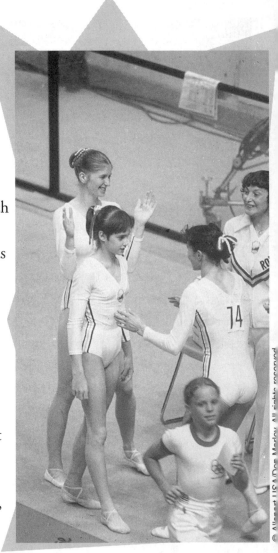

Nadia Comanici and the 1976 Romanian Olympic Team

After the fall of the Soviet Union, the Unified Team broke into separate teams such as Belarus, Russia, Ukraine, Kazakhstan, Georgia, and Uzbekistan.

The 1996 United States Olympic team

But the American women took the world by surprise at the 1996 Olympics, winning the team gold medal and breaking the long-held power of the Soviet Union. Russia earned silver at the Games and Ukraine and Belarus were fifth and sixth. It was indeed a triumph for the United States!

On the men's side, Russia earned the Olympic team titles in 1952 and 1956 but fell to the Japanese in 1960. The Japanese held onto their team title from 1960 to 1976, and the Soviet Union won again in 1980. The United States won the team title in 1984 when the Soviet-bloc countries boycotted the Games. But the Soviet Union/Russia came back strong in 1988, 1992, and 1996 to win the title again.

The male gymnasts from Russia and Japan dominated the sport of gymnastics from the 1950s through the early 1990s. Although the United States had an early start in the development of the sport, many other countries put together a unified training program and dedicated all their resources to these teams. In fact, in some countries, gymnasts leave their homes to train full-time in training centers, and they often don't see their families for years! Meanwhile, the Americans were falling behind.

It wasn't until the 1976 Olympic Games that the United States earned a historic medal in gymnastics, the first medal earned since 1932. Peter Kormann won the bronze medal on floor exercise, breaking the forty-four-year losing streak for the United States! Kormann's medal was a big break for the U.S. men. In fact, American gymnasts have earned medals in each Olympic Games since that time (with the exception of the 1980 Games, when the United States boycotted the Olympics). Kormann not only broke the dry spell for American gymnastics, but he went on to coach two other Olympians, Blaine Wilson and Kip Simons. Kormann now works for USA Gymnastics, traveling around the country and helping elite-level male gymnasts achieve their dreams.

Timothy Daggett and
Mitch Gaylord

THE HISTORY-MAKING GAMES OF 1984

The 1984 Olympics in Los Angeles marked a turning point for American gymnastics. One of the most historic moments in U.S. gymnastics occurred when the U.S. men's team won the team gold medal, the first ever for the United States' men in any international competition. The 1984 Games were also noteworthy because the

Mitch Gaylord at the 1984 Olympic Games

Soviet Union boycotted the event. It was the most successful Olympics for gymnastics in the United States. Members of the 1984 U.S. team included Peter Vidmar, Bart Conner, Tim Daggett, Mitch Gaylord, Jim Hartung, Scott Johnson, and Jim Mikus, and the team was coached by two-time Olympian Abie Grossfield. Vidmar earned the silver medal in the all-around and the gold medal on pommel horse; Conner won the gold medal on parallel bars; Daggett won the bronze medal on pommel horse; and Gaylord won the silver medal on vault and bronze medals on rings and parallel bars. And it was projected that some twenty-five million American television viewers saw the action as it unfolded.

Also at the 1984 Olympic Games, sixteen-year-old Mary Lou Retton became the Olympic all-around champion, something no American had ever done before. Her image appeared on countless commercials, magazine covers, and even the Wheaties® cereal box, making her the first female ever to grace the cover of a Wheaties box. She appeared in television shows and movies, made special public appearances, and was a commentator and a motivational speaker to people all across the United States.

The U.S. women's team earned the silver team medal and went on to win seven additional individual medals. Besides the all-around gold, Retton also won the silver medal on vault and the bronze medal on uneven bars and floor exercise. In addition, Kathy Johnson won a bronze medal on balance beam and Julianne

Mary Lou Retton at the 1984 Olympic Games

1984 U.S. Women's Olympic team

McNamara won a gold medal on uneven bars and a silver medal on floor exercise. The team included Retton, Johnson, McNamara, Tracee Talavera, Michelle Dusserre, Pam Bileck, and Marie Roethlisberger, and the team was coached by Don Peters.

Gymnastics in America exploded after those very successful 1984 Olympic Games. Kids flocked to gym clubs all across the country wanting to be the next Mary Lou Retton or Peter Vidmar! Gymnastics clubs experienced a huge jump in enrollment and business soared. This may be one of the reasons why gymnastics in America has been so strong ever since. All those kids were training hard and a large number of gymnasts were pushing one another to be the best. In nearly every Olympic Games and World Championships competition since 1984, the Americans have earned at least one medal. (The exceptions were the 1985, 1987, and 1997 World Championships.)

At the 1996 Olympic Games, the American women won the team gold medal, the first in the history of American women's gymnastics. We'll talk more about this in chapter five.

Bart Conner and Peter Vidmar

Competition Format

The format of a competition varies depending on the specifications of the International Gymnastics Federation. In the past, most competitions utilized compulsory routines, or set routines, that each gymnast must perform, and optional routines, or ones that each gymnast can make up individually using the requirements specified in the *Code of Points*. There are certain requirements, such as number of skills required, time limitations, and difficulty level. The optional routines are individually choreographed and look different from one another.

The Americans tended to neglect compulsories in the early days and concentrated instead on optional routines and difficult skills. The good thing about this is that the Americans introduced many exciting, difficult tricks to the rest of the world. The bad news is that the Americans were falling behind in compulsories, which made up half of their score. Because the Americans were weak in compulsories, they began training and competing in compulsories with more diligence. USA Gymnastics developed strategies to improve its gymnasts in the compulsory exercises. At National Championships, compulsories counted for 60 percent of the total score and optionals counted for only 40 percent of the total score. This forced gymnasts to spend more time on compulsories and, by the 1990s, the American women were the best in the world in the compulsory exercises.

Unfortunately, the compulsory routines were not nearly as exciting to watch as the optional routines, so the FIG decided to eliminate them in 1997. The United States opposed this decision because compulsories had become a strength for the Americans. It probably hurt the American women in the standings at the 1997 World Championships, which was the first major competition utilizing the new rule. The American women took sixth at this competition.

There was another major FIG rule change in 1997. The eligible age for women to compete in a World Championships or Olympic Games was raised from fifteen to sixteen. Therefore, women who were fifteen years old in 1997 were no longer eligible for the World Championships competition. Of course, each country had to deal with the new rule, so the playing field was level, but it did have a significant effect on the American performance at the 1997 World Championships. Three of the top six American women at the National Championships were not eligible to compete due to their age.

American Medalists in the Olympic Games and World Championships

1904 Olympic Games

• John Duha	Bronze	PB		• Charles Krause	Silver	RC
• George Eyser	Gold	V, PB, RC		• William Merz	Silver	SR
	Silver	PH			Bronze	PH, V
	Bronze	HB				
• Hermann Glass	Gold	SR		• Emil Voigt	Silver	IC
• Anton Heida	Gold	PH, V, HB			Bronze	SR, RC
	Silver	PB		• Ralph Wilson	Bronze	IC
• Edward Hennig	Gold	HB, IC				

1924 Olympic Games

• Frank Kriz	Gold	V

1932 Olympic Games

• Frank Cumiskey	Silver	Team		• W.G. Galbraith	Silver	RC
• Frank Haubold	Silver	Team		• Edward Gross	Silver	T
• Alfred Jochim	Silver	Team		• George Gulack	Gold	SR
• Frederick Meyer	Silver	Team		• Frank Haubold	Bronze	PH
• Raymond Bass	Gold	RC		• William Herrmann	Bronze	T
• Dallas Bixler	Gold	HB		• Alfred Jochim	Silver	V
• Edward Carmichael	Bronze	V		• William Kuhlemeier	Bronze	IC
• Tom Connelly	Bronze	RC		• George Roth	Gold	IC
• William Denton	Silver	SR		• Rowland Wolfe	Gold	T
• Phil Erenberg	Silver	IC				

1948 Olympic Games

• Laddie Bakanic	Bronze	Team		• Consetta Lenz	Bronze	Team
• Marion Barone	Bronze	Team		• Helen Schifano	Bronze	Team
• Dorothy Dalton	Bronze	Team		• Clara Schroth	Bronze	Team
• Meta Elste	Bronze	Team		• Anita Simonis	Bronze	Team

1970 World Championships

• Cathy Rigby   Silver   BB

1976 Olympic Games

• Peter Kormann   Bronze   FX

1978 World Championships

• Marcia Frederick   Gold   UB

• Kathy Johnson   Bronze   FX

• Kurt Thomas   Gold   FX

1979 World Championships

• Bart Conner	Bronze	Team		• Kurt Thomas	Bronze	Team
	Gold	PB			Gold	FX, HB
	Bronze	V			Silver	AA, PH,
• Larry Gerard	Bronze	Team				PB
• Jim Hartung	Bronze	Team		• Peter Vidmar	Bronze	Team
• Tim Lafleur	Bronze	Team		• Mike Wilson	Bronze	Team

1981 World Championships

• Julianne McNamara   Bronze   UB

• Tracee Talavera   Bronze   BB

1984 Olympic Games

• Bart Conner	Gold	Team		• Pam Bileck	Silver	Team
	Gold	PB		• Michelle Dusserre	Silver	Team
• Tim Daggett	Gold	Team		• Kathy Johnson	Silver	Team
	Bronze	PH			Bronze	BB
• Mitch Gaylord	Gold	Team		• Julianne McNamara	Silver	Team
	Silver	V			Gold	UB
	Bronze	SR, PB			Silver	FX
• Jim Hartung	Gold	Team		• Mary Lou Retton	Silver	Team
• Scott Johnson	Gold	Team			Gold	AA
• Jim Mikus	Gold	Team			Silver	V
• Peter Vidmar	Gold	Team			Bronze	UB, FX
	Gold	PH		• Marie Roethlisberger	Silver	Team
	Silver	AA		• Tracee Talavera	Silver	Team

1988 Olympic Games

• Phoebe Mills	Bronze	BB

1989 World Championships

• Brandy Johnson	Silver	V

1991 World Championships

• Michelle Campi	Silver	Team		• Kerri Strug	Silver	Team
• Hilary Grivich	Silver	Team		• Sandy Woolsey	Silver	Team
• Shannon Miller	Silver	Team		• Kim Zmeskal	Silver	Team
	Silver	UB			Gold	AA
• Betty Okino	Silver	Team			Bronze	FX
	Bronze	BB				

1992 World Championships

- Betty Okino   Silver   UB
- Kim Zmeskal   Gold   BB, FX

1992 Olympic Games

• Wendy Bruce	Bronze	Team		• Betty Okino	Bronze	Team
• Michelle Campi	Bronze	Team		• Kerri Strug	Bronze	Team
• Dominique Dawes	Bronze	Team		• Kim Zmeskal	Bronze	Team
• Shannon Miller	Bronze	Team		• Trent Dimas	Gold	HB
	Silver	AA, BB				
	Bronze	UB, FX				

1993 World Championships

- Dominique Dawes   Silver   UB, BB
- Shannon Miller   Gold   AA, UB, FX

1994 World Championships

• Amanda Borden	Silver	Team		• Shannon Miller	Silver	Team
• Amy Chow	Silver	Team			Gold	AA, BB
• Dominique Dawes	Silver	Team		• Jaycie Phelps	Silver	Team
• Larissa Fontaine	Silver	Team		• Kerri Strug	Silver	Team
				• Paul O'Neill	Silver	SR

NOTE: Separate World Championships were held for team and individual events in 1994.

1995 World Championships

• Mary Beth Arnold	Bronze	Team		• Jaycie Phelps	Bronze	Team
• Theresa Kulikowski	Bronze	Team		• Kerri Strug	Bronze	Team
• Shannon Miller	Bronze	Team		• Doni Thompson	Bronze	Team
• Dominique Moceanu	Bronze	Team				
	Silver	BB				

1996 World Championships

• Dominique Dawes	Bronze	BB

1996 Olympic Games

• Amanda Borden	Gold	Team		• Dominique Moceanu	Gold	Team
• Amy Chow	Gold	Team		• Jaycie Phelps	Gold	Team
	Silver	UB		• Kerri Strug	Gold	Team
• Dominique Dawes	Gold	Team		• Jair Lynch	Silver	PB
	Bronze	FX				
• Shannon Miller	Gold	Team				
	Gold	BB				

Key:

FX-floor exercise
PH-pommel horse
SR-still rings
V-vault
PB-parallel bars
HB-horizontal bar
UB-uneven bars
BB-balance beam
AA-all-around
IC*-Indian clubs
RC*-rope climb
T*-tumbling
*No longer an Olympic event

CHAPTER 4

EVENTS AND EQUIPMENT

Women's artistic gymnastics competitive events include vault (side horse), uneven parallel bars, balance beam, and floor exercise. The men's artistic gymnastics competitive events include floor exercise, pommel horse, still rings, vault (long horse), parallel bars, and horizontal bar. In addition, there is an all-around competition, where the four event scores for women and the six event scores for men are added together to determine the all-around score.

Top gymnasts in the world, known as elite gymnasts, compete on each event during a competition. There are only approximately 150 females at any given time who train as elite gymnasts. Elite gymnasts train around twenty-five to thirty-five hours per week. They are mentally as well as physically fit and usually don't have a lot of extra time for extracurricular activities other than gymnastics. Some elite gymnasts go to a normal school and may be released early to train, while others are homeschooled or attend private schools so that they can train more hours in the gym. Either way, these individuals are very dedicated and goal-oriented.

The gymnasts compete on the apparatus in Olympic order, which is vault, uneven parallel bars, balance beam, and floor exercise for the women; and floor exercise, pommel horse, still rings, vault, parallel bars, and horizontal bar for the men.

A team event is usually held at major competitions such as the Olympic Games and World Championships. Depending on the format of the competition, which is dictated by the International Gymnastics Federation, the number of gymnasts who make up a team may vary. At the 1997 World Championships in Lausanne, Switzerland, six gymnasts made up a team, five gymnasts competed on each event, and four scores counted toward the team score. Therefore, if you have one gymnast who is exceptionally strong on one or two events but not so strong on the other events, you may elect not to compete this gymnast on her weak events. The coach uses strategy to put a team together to achieve the most success.

Obviously, the gymnasts who do not compete in all the events are not eligible for an all-around award.

At the 1996 Olympic Games, there were seven gymnasts on a team, six gymnasts competed on each event, and the five highest scores counted toward the team score.

Julianne McNamara on uneven bars

A gymnast competes on one event at a time and salutes the judges of the event prior to starting her routine. One of the judges will raise a green flag to let the gymnast know the judging panel is ready for her to compete. After the routine is complete, the gymnast will again acknowledge the judges by saluting and will march back to her designated area. The judges then post the gymnast's score on a scoreboard or scoreflasher and rotate it for all to see.

The Rule Book

The *Code of Points* is the rule book for elite gymnastics and was created by the International Gymnastics Federation. All the top gymnasts in the world use this rule book to create routines on all the events. The *Code of Points* is updated every four years, right after the Olympic Games, to reflect changes taking place in gymnastics. The *Code of Points* is a guide to the scoring of the sport of gymnastics. It tells the gymnasts and coaches what each skill is rated and gives the name of the skill.

If a gymnast successfully competes a skill for the first time at a World Championships or Olympic Games and submits the skill to be evaluated by the judges, the skill could be named after the gymnast and printed in the next *Code of Points*. The "Thomas," for example, was named after Kurt Thomas, and the "Miller," after Shannon Miller. In fact, many American gymnasts have skills named after them!

Once the *Code of Points* is updated, it must be translated into different languages so that gymnasts, coaches, and judges all over the world can read and understand the rules. This is a complicated process because some terms are hard to translate. There are actually people who specialize in translating gymnastics terminology!

The Women's Events

VAULT

The vault, sometimes called the horse, still remains a vivid memory of many who watched the 1996 Olympic Games.

Here's the scene: Dominique Moceanu was second to last on vault—the last rotation for the Americans—and she fell on both vaults. Kerri Strug was the last gymnast to compete on vault, and knew she had to hit in order to win the team gold medal. If she didn't, the Americans would have had to count a low score in their team total, allowing the Russian team to edge into first place. Strug ran down the runway, but she, too, fell on her first vault. Strug injured her ankle when she fell, and limped down the runway for her second and final vault. Strug knew this was the last chance for the Americans to win the gold. She ran down the runway as fast as she could on the injured ankle, and landed the vault! She scored high enough to secure a gold medal for the U.S. Olympic team. She had to be carried onto the awards platform by her coach, Bela Karolyi.

The vision of Strug running down that runway, landing her vault, and then falling down clutching her ankle has remained in the minds of millions who watched this moment in gymnastics history, and it has made her a hero.

Speed, power, and courage are important attributes to have when vaulting. Top-level gymnasts appear to fly through the air when they vault. They make it look much easier than it really is!

The women's vault is 120 centimeters high for elite competitors (the horse height varies depending on the age and ability level of the gymnast), 35 centimeters wide, and 160 centimeters long. The runway is 1 meter wide and a maximum of 25 meters long. The vault is placed sideways with the board in front of the vault. (For the men, the horse

Kerri Strug will always be remembered for her heroic vault in the 1996 Olympic Games

is placed lengthwise to accommodate the physical size difference between male and female gymnasts.)

The springboard is also called a Reuther board, after the man who created it. It uses a springlike device to help gymnasts jump to the horse. The board is four feet long and three feet wide. Gymnasts place the board at a comfortable distance from the horse, usually depending on the type of vault the gymnast is trying and the size and ability level of the gymnast.

The vault is made of a combination of wood and steel, wrapped with padding and covered with leather or a synthetic material. The covering has a nonskid surface.

The landing area is set up on the opposite side of the horse with mats.

The key to vaulting is the run. A gymnast must run fast with long strides to gain enough momentum to hit the board and execute the vault successfully. Usually the faster the run, the better the vault. Many gymnastics coaches bring in track-and-field coaches to work with their gymnasts on running speed and form to improve vaulting and tumbling.

Vaults are divided into four families: 1) handsprings (cartwheels); 2) forward saltos (with and without twists); 3) backward saltos (with or without twists); and 4) round-off entry vaults (the gymnast performs a cartwheel onto the board and takes off backward to land on the horse). When competing, female gymnasts get two vaults.

Beginners in the sport will do drills for running, hurdling onto the board, and entry-level vaults like the squat vault, straddle vault, and handspring vault.

The preflight is the first part of the vault—from the time your feet hit the board to the time when your hands hit the horse. The judges begin evaluating a vault in its preflight. (Keep in mind the judges don't evaluate the run.)

The next step in the vault is the repulsion, where you try to turn your speed and power into height. Repulsion is what happens immediately after your hands hit the vault. You try to rise as high as you can off the horse.

Next is the afterflight, which is everything that happens after the gymnast hits the vault, including the landing.

Of course, the last part is the landing, when your feet hit the mat. The best scenario is to "stick" the landing, which means land on the mat without having to take any steps. At meets you'll hear teammates yell "Stick it!" to one another, to encourage a perfect landing. Many times a gymnast will have to take a step or two or a hop to gain her balance. If so, the judge will make the appropriate deductions—one tenth per step—in the gymnast's score.

To determine the final score, the judge adds up the deductions and subtracts the difficulty rating of the vault. (See chapter 3 for more about scoring.)

The best part about the vaulting event is that gymnasts typically learn one or maybe two vaults, and then spend time perfecting the skill. On other events, there are many skills to learn and perfect, so the gymnasts spend less time on each one. But the vault tends to take less time to learn, so more emphasis can be placed on perfecting the skill.

UNEVEN PARALLEL BARS

The uneven parallel bars have changed a great deal over the last fifty years. Gymnasts used to stop on the bar and do poses and scales while standing on the low bar and holding onto the high bar. This type of routine was replaced with a smooth, flowing variation. Gymnasts would beat or wrap the bar, which means they would hang from the high bar and wrap around the low bar where their hips bend. The bars were fairly close together to allow the gymnasts' hips to reach the lower bar. Now most bars are spread far apart so that the gymnasts can swing and flip around the high bar without hitting their hips on the low bar.

Uneven parallel bars

Many skills created for the men's horizontal bar have been transferred to the women's uneven parallel bars. However, it's a little more challenging to do the skills on the women's bars because there are two bars instead of one—and the

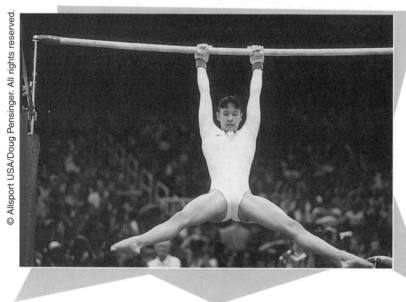

Amy Chow is recognized as one of the world's best on the bars.

gymnast has to make sure she doesn't hit the second bar. Skills such as the giant swings, Gienger, Deltchev, and Gaylord were first done by men but have been incorporated into women's gymnastics.

The low bar height for international competition is 148 centimeters, the high bar height is 228 centimeters, and the maximum space between the bars is 100–150 centimeters. The bars used to be made of wood but would often splinter and break. Now the bars are made of fiberglass with a thin veneer of wood. The fiberglass makes the bars stronger and more flexible to allow the gymnast to execute turns and flips.

When circling around the bars, many gymnasts' hands become hot and may blister and tear, which is called a rip. When this happens, or sometimes before this happens, gymnasts wear hand guards or grips to protect their hands. The gymnasts' hands will eventually build up a protective layer of callouses and will not rip frequently.

The uneven parallel bars demand upper body strength as well as concentration, courage, coordination, and split-second timing.

During competition, the bar routine should flow smoothly from one movement to the next without pauses, extra swings, or additional supports. The elite routine must move from the low bar to the high bar, incorporating grip changes, releases and regrasps, flight elements, changes of direction, saltos, and circle swings through the handstand position. A bar routine usually has ten to twelve elements included, and elite-level gymnasts are required to have two release skills, in which the gymnast lets go of the bar completely and then regrasps it. Although there is no time limit, it usually takes the gymnast twenty to thirty seconds to complete her bar routine.

Beginner gymnasts will work on strength exercises such as pull-ups, chin-ups, leg lifts, and glides. The gymnast will also work on hip pullovers, where she is standing on the ground and pulls her body around the bar to end up in a front support position (hips and hands on the bar with head up). The gymnast may also work on back hip circles, sole circles, and mill circles. (Don't worry if this all

Falling off the bars

If a gymnast falls from the bars, there is an automatic half-point deduction, but she is allowed to get back on and continue her routine.

seems foreign and difficult to you—a gymnastics coach can explain these skills and help you learn them.)

The glide kip is probably one of the most difficult skills to learn. You may have to try hundreds of times before you can make the glide kip by yourself. Then, once you do it, you'll wonder why it took you so long to learn!

Many gymnasts claim uneven bars is their favorite event. It's fun to swing around the bars and feel a sense of accomplishment as you learn new skills.

BALANCE BEAM

The best gymnasts on beam make it look easy, like they're working on floor exercise. In fact, that's the key to this event—making it look like you're on the floor, rather than on a four-inch-wide beam. The beam stands approximately four feet high and sixteen feet long, allowing for tumbling and dance passes (although depending on the age and ability level of the gymnast, the height of the beam may be lowered).

The balance beam event requires concentration, flexibility, grace, rhythm, tumbling, good body position, and above all, confidence.

Good body position means having good posture and not slouching. When working the beam, the gymnast must stand tall, lift up in her ribs, and keep her back straight, head aligned, and body balanced on both sides. You've probably heard someone say, "Stand up tall and don't slouch." This is exactly what gymnasts strive to do when working on the beam. Dance training helps to achieve the good body posture that is so important, especially on the beam.

The beam routine lasts between seventy to ninety seconds and a deduction is taken if the routine is too short or too long. The judge will ring a bell at one minute twenty seconds to let the gymnast know she has ten seconds to complete her dismount from the beam.

The gymnast must cover the entire area of the beam during her routine, plus move high above the beam, down low on the beam, and side to side. The gymnast must use acrobatic, gymnastic, and dance movements to create high points, or peaks, in the exercise. There are more specific requirements depending on the level of competition. For example, elite gymnasts have special requirements on the beam such as: one acrobatic series, including at least two flight elements; a turn on one leg of at least 360 degrees; a gymnastics leap or jump with great amplitude; one gymnastics/acrobatics series; one gymnastics series; and one element close to the beam.

An example of an acrobatic series is flip-flop, flip-flop, layout salto. An example of a gymnastics series is a turn followed by a split jump.

Gymnasts should show variations in rhythm, changes in

Julianne McNamara on the beam

level, and a blend of gymnastics and acrobatic elements. The gymnast should not wiggle, wobble, or stop during the routine.

There is an automatic half-point deduction for falling off the beam.

Beginning gymnasts will start with the basics such as walking forward, backward, and sideways. They will move up to runs, hops, jumps, leaps, rolls, handstands, and cartwheels. Before mastering an element on the beam, the gymnast should have mastered the skill on the floor. Gymnasts start out learning skills on the low beam and gradually increase the height until they can successfully accomplish the skill on the high beam.

When learning a new skill you may be able to put a beam pad on the beam to widen and soften the beam. The beam pad is a soft mat fitted around the beam so that if you're a little off, you'll land on the beam pad instead of on the floor. Once you have mastered the skill with the beam pad, the coach will take it off so that you can master the skill on the four-inch-wide beam.

The balance beam has come a long way over the years. It used to be made of wood and was a little slippery. Now the balance beam is topped with a foam pad and tightly covered with a nonskid material, usually suede leather or a synthetic fabric. The beam is even a little soft and springy now, allowing gymnasts to do difficult flips and twists that were unheard of just twenty to thirty years ago. The beam rests on an adjustable steel base.

Balance beam is probably the most difficult event for most gymnasts because of the concentration necessary to achieve success. Many gymnasts get nervous on the beam, lose concentration, and shake, which causes them to fall off. It's difficult to focus and concentrate during a competition when your mom, dad, sister, brother, aunt, uncle, grandma, coach, and judge are watching! The best gymnast puts all the distractions aside and performs her routine like she does in practice, concentrating on each and every move.

FLOOR EXERCISE

This event combines dance and tumbling with music to showcase an entertaining and creative routine. The floor routine must be choreographed to music and lasts between seventy to ninety seconds.

Music can range from show tunes to classical to pop, and should showcase the gymnast's best features. For example, very graceful gymnasts (most of whom have had a long and successful ballet background) will probably do best with classical music. On the other hand, gymnasts with less dance experience may opt for more jazzy or popular music. It's a personal preference left up to the gymnast and her coach.

Although men and women both compete on floor exercise, the men's routine focuses on power and strength rather than the power and grace of the women's routines. Also, men's floor exercise routines are not performed to music.

Both men and women compete on a floor exercise mat that is forty feet by forty feet, with a two-foot-wide border all the way around that is considered out of bounds. The gymnast must cover the entire area of the mat. The gymnastics elements should flow freely into each other, while the leaps and tumbling should cover distance, and the pirouettes and turns should add excitement to the routine.

The gymnast must use acrobatic and gymnastic elements to create high points in the exercise. For the elite competitors, these include two acrobatic series, one with at least two or more saltos in different directions; an acrobatic/gymnastics series; and a gymnastics series. The gymnast must harmoniously blend these elements throughout while making use of floor space, changing both direction and level of movement.

The first tumbling pass in a gymnast's routine is called the mount, and the last pass is called the dismount. Elite-level gymnasts have between three and five tumbling passes in their routines.

Floor exercise is usually considered a favorite event of many gymnasts because they are able to have some fun and play to the judges and crowd. They are able to show their personality on this event more so than on the other three events.

On floor exercise, gymnasts must have the power to execute tumbling passes; the grace to manage the leaps, turns, and jumps; and the finesse to put it all together!

Beginners will learn rolls, cartwheels, handstands, bridges, walkovers, flip-flops (or back hand-springs), front handsprings, aerials, saltos, and other skills.

Once a gymnast makes a team, her coach may suggest or require that she take a dance class. Dance is an important component of a floor routine. Along with dance comes flexibility. It's important for gymnasts to have

Olga Korbut won the world's adoration with her floor exercise routine

Parallel bars

flexibility in their legs in order to execute split leaps and other dance elements.

The floor exercise event was competed on a wood floor some thirty years ago. Later gymnasts were allowed to place small panel mats in the corners where they planned to do their tumbling. This didn't allow the gymnasts to get too daring in their skills since landings were very dangerous. When full floor exercise mats (forty feet by forty feet) came along, the gymnasts were allowed to perform much more difficult skills. Further skill advancement occurred when the spring floor was introduced. A spring floor is just what its name describes, a firm floor exercise mat with springs underneath to give the gymnast a little extra power. The spring floor is built from plywood sheets and a layer of rubber, foam, or springs. It is topped with a soft elastic material, such as rubber, and covered with carpet.

A spring floor allows the gymnasts to compete very difficult skills. For example, at the 1987 European Championships, the Soviet Union's Valeri Liukin competed the first triple back salto on floor exercise in men's gymnastics. Since this time, a handful of other male gymnasts have also competed the skill. In 1998, Kristen Maloney was the first American woman to successfully compete a double layout with a full twist.

What used to be difficult many years ago is now elementary for top gymnasts, primarily due to the advances made in equipment and training in the sport.

The Men's Events

The men's artistic gymnastics events include floor exercise, pommel horse, still rings, vault, parallel bars, and horizontal bar.

The floor exercise routines consist of dynamic tumbling skills, balance elements, and transitional or gymnastics skills performed between tumbling passes. Unlike the women, the men do not perform their floor exercise routine to music. However, both the

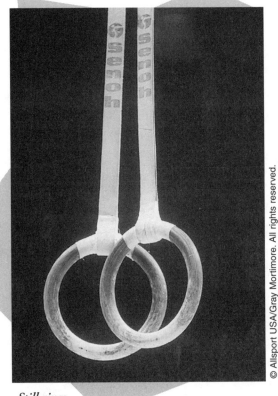

Still rings

men and the women must cover the entire area of the floor exercise during their routine.

During a pommel horse routine, the gymnast must cover all three areas of the horse—the middle and both ends—while performing continuous circular movements interrupted only by the required scissors elements. The only part of the body that should touch the pommel horse is the hands. This event takes extreme upper body strength!

Still rings also take a lot of upper body strength and flexibility, especially in the shoulders. Gymnasts swing into handstands by using front and back swings. The gymnast must also include an element of strength and hold it for at least two seconds. The object of still rings is to keep the rings very still! This is difficult to accomplish, especially when combining strength and swing elements.

On vault, the men turn the horse lengthwise, whereas the women turn the horse sideways. Another difference in the men's and women's vault is that the men get to vault only once and the women get to vault twice. Other than these two major differences, the rest of the men's vault event is nearly the same as the women's.

Pommel horse

Parallel bars are two bars placed side by side. Routines consist of swing and flight elements. Strength parts may be used, although they are not required, and there is a limit on the number of stops or hold parts during the routine. At the upper level of the sport, the gymnasts are required to perform a release move, a skill in which both hands release and regrasp the bars.

Horizontal bar is probably the most daring and exciting of the men's events. This event is similar to the women's uneven parallel bars in that gymnasts swing around the bar, change grip and body position, and do release moves. The men's horizontal bar (sometimes called high bar) is higher than the women's high bar. The rail is also much smaller.

Other Gymnastics Equipment

If you hang around a gymnastics facility for any period of time, you'll probably hear about or see some of the following items.

CHALK

Chalk is used on the hands by women gripping the uneven parallel bars, and by men for the pommel horse, still rings, parallel bars, and horizontal bar. Chalk is a white powdery substance that is really magnesium carbonate.

Dominique Moceanu applying chalk before competing

Some gymnasts prefer a lot of chalk, some like no chalk, and others like a mixture of chalk and water to make their grip sticky. To each her own preference!

It's funny to sit back at a major international competition and watch gymnasts from some countries pack the bars with chalk and water while gymnasts from other countries use sandpaper to remove the chalk before they mount the equipment. It truly is a personal preference!

GRIPS

You can't talk about chalk and bars without mentioning grips. Grips are worn on some gymnasts' hands during their performance. Many gymnasts have callouses on their hands that can rip open and bleed, making hanging onto the bar painful. Therefore, the gymnast may elect to wear grips.

MATS

Another necessity in the sport of gymnastics is mats. Mats are used under all the pieces of apparatus as a safety precaution for the gymnasts. Mats are specifically made to fit under each piece of equipment. There's a special mat that fits under the beam, a special mat that fits under the bars, and a special mat that fits at the end of the vault.

Mats have come a long way thanks to much research and development to ensure that the best surface is available to gymnasts.

Some mats are created for use in practice only and not in a competition. These mats are much thicker, allowing the gymnast to safely land on a soft mat while trying new skills. However, these types of mats make sticking the landings (when a gymnast lands a routine and doesn't move) more difficult to achieve.

There's even a special vaulting mat that fits between the board and the horse for executing a round-off entry vault, called a Yurchenko. This keeps the gymnast safe if she fails to hit the board in the correct position.

TRAMPOLINE

Of course you've heard of the trampoline and you have probably even jumped on one. Trampolines are great tools for gymnasts to learn flipping and twisting skills. Most gyms have at least one trampoline. Some gyms have an in-ground trampoline, which means there's a big hole in the ground and the trampoline fits in the hole so that it is almost even with the ground. This alleviates the fear of falling off the trampoline. Many coaches spot, or stand nearby, ready to help gymnasts on the trampoline when they attempt a flipping or twisting skill, or they put the gymnast in a spotting belt. However, beginners must perfect a large number of elements before learning to flip. Coaches will teach beginners how to jump and stop, tuck jump, straddle jump, pike jump, seat drop, jump half-turn, jump full-turn, and much more.

TUMBLE TRAMPOLINE

This piece of equipment is fairly new in gyms across the country. It's like a trampoline, but it's long and narrow in shape and is used for tumbling. The tumble trampoline allows the gymnasts to tumble but alleviates the hard surface of a regular mat. It's a great learning tool for tumbling skills.

PITS

There are three types of pits: a solid foam pit, loose foam pit, and bungee pit. The purpose of the pit is to allow gymnasts to try difficult skills and land safely. In other words, a pit is used as a training aid for gymnasts.

The solid foam pit is like a big, giant mat, and the loose foam pit is like a swimming pool filled with thousands of pieces of foam. The bungee pit is relatively new, with only a few in existence throughout the United States. The bungee pit also has the pieces of foam, but the system has a net or bed and bungee system in place underneath the foam. The benefit of the bungee pit is that the foam does not pack as easily as the loose foam, so it can be safer.

However, no matter which pit system is being used, gymnasts should still beware. Injuries can, and do, still occur in a pit. Gymnasts must take caution to land properly. Never land headfirst, on your face or chest, or with your back arched. Also, be sure you don't jump on someone who is still in the pit!

CHAPTER 5

NATIONAL AND INTERNATIONAL COMPETITIONS

—★—

The United States hosts several major gymnastics events each year. These include the Reese's International Gymnastics Cup, the Visa American Cup, the International 3 on 3 Gymnastics Championships, the International Team Championships, the World Championships and Olympic Trials, and the John Hancock U.S. Gymnastics Championships.

Of course, there are many other national elite competitions including the American Classic, Winter Cup Challenge, U.S. Classic, U.S. Olympic Festivals, National Gymnastics Festival, and other competitions.

The American Cup is the most established competition. This event has been in existence since 1976, when America's Bart Conner and Romania's Nadia Comanici won the premier event. The event has been going strong ever since! This international invitational includes gymnasts from fifteen to twenty-five countries, depending on the year and the invitations sent by USA Gymnastics. The athletes compete in a preliminary round of competition during day one and the top eight advance to the all-around finals on day two. The top all-around gymnasts for men and women win the coveted American Cup! Many American Cup champions have gone on to win World and Olympic medals, including Kerri Strug, Dominique Dawes, Vitaly Scherbo,

Shannon Miller, Kim Zmeskal, Betty Okino, Trent Dimas, Brandy Johnson, Phoebe Mills, Tim Daggett, Peter Vidmar, and Mary Lou Retton, just to name a few.

The International 3 on 3 Gymnastics Championships has a unique and fun format, which was developed in order to gain more exposure for rhythmic gymnastics. This event combines a men's artistic gymnast, a women's artistic gymnast, and a rhythmic gymnast to form a trio. Each member of the trio competes on an event of his or her choice and the scores are combined to get a team total. The top teams advance to round two, where the winning trio is awarded.

The International Team Championships is an international team competition. The United States invites one or two of the top teams in the world. No all-around or individual awards are given, only team awards. The best thing about this event is that it usually includes junior and senior competition, so the juniors get the opportunity to gain valuable experience. The junior women are fifteen and under and the senior women are sixteen and up.

Watch the best in the world . . . live!

To get a complete list of gymnastics events, dates, and locations, contact USA Gymnastics at:
(317) 237-5050;

or write to:
USA Gymnastics
Pan American Plaza
201 South Capitol Avenue
Suite 300
Indianapolis, IN 46225;

or visit their website at:
http://www.usa-gymnastics.org

At the 1998 International Team Championships, the senior women, led by Kristen Maloney, won the title over China and Romania. The junior women, led by eleven-year-old Ashley Postell, took second behind China.

The Pan American Championships and the Pan American Games are two more high-level international events. Countries that have a member federation in the Pan American Gymnastics Union are invited to participate in both of these events. In a four-year cycle, called a quadrennium, the Pan American Championships

Rhythmic gymnasts use balls, hoops, ribbon, and other apparatus in their routines

(senior competition) take place the first year, the Junior Pan American Championships occur the next, the Pan American Games (senior competition) take place the third year, and the cycle concludes with the Junior Pan American Championships the last year. There are twenty-three countries included in the Pan American Gymnastics Union including Argentina, Barbados, Bermuda, Bolivia, Brazil, Canada, Chile, Colombia, Costa Rica, Cuba, Dominican Republic, Ecuador,

El Salvador, Guatemala, Honduras, Mexico, Paraguay, Panama, Peru, Puerto Rico, United States, Uruguay, and Venezuela.

The National Championships competition is probably the most important event for American gymnasts each year. This is where the top athletes in the all-around make the USA National Team. The number of athletes placed on the National Team varies, depending on the year. USA Gymnastics predetermines the number of athletes that will make up the National Team. It's usually fourteen to twenty seniors and twelve to twenty juniors. Once a gymnast makes the National Team, she is eligible to travel both nationally and internationally competing on behalf of the United States. The National Team athletes receive competition apparel and some type of funding, depending on the year and the placement of the gymnast. Gymnasts who are maintaining their NCAA eligibility and want to compete on a collegiate gymnastics team have to be careful about accepting money. These athletes have to follow the NCAA rules.

The USA Gymnastics Women's Program Committee makes the assignments of which athletes go to which competitions. There are many international competitions held throughout the year, such as the Chunichi Cup in Japan, the Swiss Cup in Switzerland, the DTB Pokal in Germany, and the Canberra Cup in Australia, just to name a few. For the big events, such as the World Championships or Olympic Games, there is usually a trials competition to determine who will make up the team.

The World Championships and Olympic Trials determine which gymnasts will make the World Championships or Olympic Games teams. These events are usually held approximately three weeks prior to the big event to ensure that the best athletes are on the team. Many gymnasts say that they experience more pressure from the Trials event than the actual World Championships or Olympic Games competitions.

Did you know . . .

the John Hancock Tour of World Gymnastics Champions, which included members of the men's, women's and rhythmic American gymnastics Olympic teams and invited guests, visited 34 cities at the end of 1996 and was seen by approximately 450,000 spectators? The tour also visited 23 cities in early 1997 and an additional 33 cities in late 1997.

The World Championships competition, in terms of size, is the largest of all the events. At the 1997 World Championships in Lausanne, Switzerland, there were thirty-five men's teams and nineteen women's teams competing in the event. With six athletes, a coach, an assistant coach, and a trainer per team on the floor, there were 144 individuals on the women's side and 315 on the men's!

The FIG sets the schedule for the World Championships and the format of the competition. For example, from 1992 to 1996 there were six World Championships held, two in 1994. Some of the World Championships are individual event competitions only; some are full-scale events with team, all-around, and individual events awarded; and some are all-around and individual event competitions only.

The Olympics is the biggest event in terms of prestige. Only the top twelve men's teams, the top twelve women's teams, and the top all-around competitors in the world qualify to compete in the Olympic Games. So, although there are not as many partici-pants, they are the best in the world!

Because the Summer Olympics occur only once every four years, there is a great amount of prestige and honor associated with the Olympic Games, not to mention a worldwide audience!

The last Olympic Games were held in Atlanta, Georgia, in 1996. This was the first time since 1984 that the United States had hosted the event. The next Olympic Games in the year 2000 will be held in Sydney, Australia. The 2004 Games have not yet been awarded.

Nearly all the events listed above enjoy network television exposure and have contributed to the popularity of the sport of gymnastics in America.

A major gymnastics event may even come to your city in the future. If it does, ask your parents to get tickets. The events are a lot of fun to watch. You'll even get to see Tumbles, the official USA Gymnastics mascot!

Most fans who see their first gymnastics competition in person say, "Wow, those gymnasts sure are small and talented." The gymnasts tend to look larger when they're on television!

Junior Olympic Competitions

In addition to the major competitions listed above, there are thousands of USA Gymnastics Junior Olympic competitions that involve approximately 70,000 gymnasts in the United States. These competitions occur throughout the year all across the country.

Although the FIG dropped compulsories for the elite athletes, the USA Gymnastics Junior Olympic Program utilizes compulsory routines in its beginning levels. The routines are developed or modified once every four years. The Junior Olympic Program is a developmental program that is divided into four major segments.

The developmental Levels 1 through 4 consist of short sequences of elements. These routines were designed to be noncompetitive and achievement-oriented for use within a gym's pre-team program; however, Level 4 may also be used as an introductory competitive program. Many states even hold a Level 4 State Championships competition.

The second part consists of compulsory Levels 5 and 6. Both of these levels are progressive in nature, building upon the skills required at the previous level. Competitive opportunities are provided up to and including the USA Gymnastics State Championships.

The third part is Level 7, which consists of compulsory elements put together in an optional format. This level is designed to bridge the gap between compulsory routines and optional routines. This level also provides competitive opportunities up to and including the State Championships.

The fourth and final segment is the optional Levels 8, 9, and 10. These levels have modifications to the FIG requirements for each event and have additional competitive opportunities provided for the gymnasts. Level 10 season concludes at the Junior Olympic National Championships, Level 9 at the Eastern or Western Championships, and Level 8 at the Regional Championships.

The Junior Olympic Program gives you a solid foundation of basic skills in order to advance safely. The program allows you to advance at your own pace. One gymnast may progress from Level 5 to Level 6 in one competitive season while another gymnast may take two or three seasons to move from Level 5 to Level 6.

There are separate age divisions within each level so an eight-year-old doesn't have to compete with a twelve-year-old at the same level. Rather, the age divisions for Level 6 are seven to eleven, twelve to fourteen, and fifteen and up.

Most of these types of events take place in a local gymnastics club or at a junior high or high school gymnasium.

Many of the USA Gymnastics member organizations operate and conduct their own gymnastics competition formats. Member organizations have the right to modify the rules of the Junior Olympic Program and use them to meet the needs of their athletes. For example, the Special Olympics modifies the Junior Olympic rules and conducts events all across the country for their Special Olympians.

Other groups that conduct competitions include the Amateur Athletic Union, National High School Association, National Collegiate Athletic Association, American Turners, and American Sokols, to name a few.

Many gymnasts think that competitions are the best part about the sport. They enjoy competing with other gymnasts and striving to reach their goals. Gymnasts' goals may be to win the meet, to earn a medal, or simply to stay on that balance beam.

How Are These Events Judged?

What are the judges looking for in each event and how do they arrive at a score? At national- and international-level competitions, there are four to six judges at each event. Two judges determine the start value based on difficulties and bonuses met. The remaining judges deduct for execution and composition only. Each judge arrives at a score independently. The high and the

Nadia Comanici scored the Olympics' first perfect ten

A Perfect 10!

The highest score a gymnast can receive on her vault, uneven bars, balance beam, and/or floor exercise routine is a 10. A score of 10 would indicate that the routine was perfect!

low scores are tossed out, and the remaining scores are averaged.

During each routine, the gymnast begins with less than a perfect 10 score. For women, the gymnast starts with a 9.00 while men start at an 8.60. Judges make deductions for errors in execution and for any missing requirements in composition of the routine.

The judge may award bonus points, up to 1 for the women and 1.40 for the men. So, if a gymnast hits a perfect routine, including bonus points added, he or she will score a perfect 10.

In elite-level competition, gymnastic skills are divided into five levels of difficulty ranging from A (the easiest skills) to E (the most difficult skills). Each routine must have a minimum number of parts, dictated by the FIG *Code of Points.*

In the Junior Olympic Program, there are two to four judges per event. If two judges are evaluating the routine, the scores are averaged together to get the final score. If there are four judges, then the high and low scores are thrown out and the middle two scores are averaged.

There is a Junior Olympic Program Manual that lists specific deductions taken for each routine at each level. In general, judges take deductions for bent legs, bent arms, steps on dismounts, flexed toes, wobbles on beam, lack of amplitude, falls off the apparatus, and missing elements in a routine.

Podiums

Many national and international competitions are conducted on a podium, which is a raised platform on which the equipment is placed. The podium is about four feet high off the ground and serves as a stage on which the gymnasts compete. It allows the audience a better opportunity to view the action.

Many top gymnasts don't get the opportunity to compete on the podium until they reach a major competition like the Pan American Championships, Goodwill Games, World Championships, or Olympic Games. In 1995, USA Gymnastics made a commitment to utilize a podium setup for all of its major events such as the Reese's Cup, American Cup, International Team Championships,

The Podium

The main rule for the podium is that only the gymnast is allowed on the podium during her routine. The coach may pull her board after the mount or stand close during a release move but is supposed to leave the podium as soon as possible. At the 1988 Olympic Games, American gymnast Rhonda Faehn pulled the board for her teammate after she mounted. Rhonda sat on the podium and watched her teammate finish the routine. Madame Ellen Berger, FIG women's technical director, took a technical deduction of .5 from the team score, insisting that Rhonda had violated the "no coaches on the podium" rule. The American team lost the bronze medal to East Germany by .3.

National Championships, and World Championships or Olympic Trials. This has helped the athletes get familiar with competing on the podium. Many gymnasts say the feel of competing up on the podium is a little different than competing on the regular floor. Having the opportunity to compete on the podium prior to a major gymnastics competition gives the American athletes a slight advantage over some of their competitors, who may not have experienced the podium environment.

Apparel

So, what do top gymnasts wear to competitions? The women wear a leotard. The leotard has gone through many changes over the years. No longer are leotards a single color with a scoop neck and a low cut around the thighs. The latest trend in uniforms is neon bright colors, stripes, and wild patterns. Another trend is cutout patterns around the neck and chest region or across the back.

There could be a deduction taken if a gymnast's leotard is cut above her hip bone.

During a major team competition, each gymnast must wear the identical uniform displaying the country emblem on the chest or in another visible area. If all

Rhythmic gymnastics

Rhythmic gymnastics utilizes handheld apparatus including a ball, hoop, rope, clubs, and ribbon. Rhythmic gymnastics first became an Olympic sport in 1984 and is relatively new to the United States. Rhythmic gymnastics is very popular in Europe, sometimes attracting more spectators than artistic gymnastics competitions. There are approximately 1,500 to 2,000 girls competing in rhythmic gymnastics in the United States.

members of the team are not dressed identically, a deduction could be taken from the team score.

Gymnasts wear pants and jackets over their leotards to keep them warm when marching onto the competition floor and rotating from event to event during the competition. Most gymnasts also wear their pants and jackets onto the awards platform to receive their medals.

The men wear competition jerseys and pants or shorts. In 1988, male gymnasts were given the option to wear different pants and shorts other than the standard white. This allowed the male uniform to be much more versatile. Now, many male gymnasts wear sleek, multicolored spandex pants and either solid or striped shorts.

In 1991, the FIG approved the use of commercial signage or logos on uniforms. Only one sign or logo is allowed per item of apparel and it must be in a designated location on the uniform.

Everywhere you look there is advertising—television, radio, magazines, billboards—and now it is prevalent in the sport of gymnastics. You've heard of walking advertisements—gymnasts have become flipping advertisements!

Rhythmic uniforms

In rhythmic gymnastics, the FIG approved that the gymnasts could wear either leotards or unitards, a one-piece uniform that covers them from the chest to the ankles. The reason the FIG approved the unitard is because in some countries women are not allowed to show their legs. Now gymnasts from these countries can compete in rhythmic gymnastics. This change has not been accepted in women's artistic gymnastics.

CHAPTER 6

WOMEN GYMNASTS FROM AROUND THE WORLD

Olga Korbut

Each time a new Olympic Champion is crowned, a dramatic increase in interest develops in the sport of gymnastics. Olga Korbut was the first gymnast to revolutionize the sport. As one journalist put it, "You couldn't sell a thousand tickets to a gymnastics event before Olga, and now arenas sell out to see Olga perform."

It is fairly safe to say that America discovered women's gymnastics when they discovered Olga Korbut. Seventeen-year-old Olga was the first star to rise in the sport of gymnastics here in America. From the Soviet Union, Olga was a four-foot eleven-inch, eighty-five-pound dynamo with pigtails. She arrived at the 1972 Olympic Games in Munich as an alternate, but when a teammate was injured she stepped in to help out. And help out she did! She stunned viewers with her daring back flips on uneven bars and balance beam. She dazzled the world with her daring skills, pixie style, and bright smile.

The words rang out from the television set: "I don't believe it," said ABC's commentator Gordon Maddux when Olga flung herself into space while performing on the bars. "Give her an eleven!"

Olga was definitely an innovator, the one who pushed the envelope in women's gymnastics. She was the first to do a back salto on the

high bar to a regrasp, which became known as the Korbut flip. She
dazzled audiences with her layout on floor exercise to a chest roll, and
back flip on balance beam.

Olga won three gold medals at the 1972 Olympic Games including
balance beam, floor exercise, and team event. She earned the silver
medal on uneven bars, which was very controversial. The audience
thought she deserved the gold and held up competition for twenty
minutes with their protests.

Actually it was Olga's teammate, Lyudmila Tourischeva, who won the
all-around at those Olympic Games, but Olga, who finished seventh all-
around, was the one remembered for her charisma and personality. She
was the first Russian gymnast ever endeared to the American public.

During the all-around finals competition, Olga slipped from the bars
and fell. She cried and showed her emotions like no other Soviet gymnast had ever done before. Many of the 15,000 spectators and those
watching on television cried with her and loved her even more. Many
felt the sorrow and hurt she was feeling and became instant fans! In fact,

*Olga Korbut
on beam, for
which she
earned a gold
medal*

she was awarded the Associated Press Female Athlete of the Year, and in 1973 was awarded ABC's Wide World of Sports Athlete of the Year.

Olga took second in the all-around behind Tourischeva at the 1974 World Championships in Varna, Bulgaria, and earned a gold medal on vault and three silver medals on uneven bars, balance beam, and floor exercise.

Olga helped her team earn the gold medal at the 1976 Olympic Games and won the silver medal on the beam behind a new up-and-coming star, Nadia Comanici.

Olga retired from the sport in 1978 and married Leonid Bortkevich, a lead singer for a popular Soviet rock group. They had a son and eventually moved to the United States. Olga is coaching the sport she loves and helping kids in America become better gymnasts.

Nadia Comanici

Nadia, born in Onesti, Moldavia, in 1961, became a star in 1976 at the Olympic Games in Montreal, competing for her home country of Romania. This eighty-six-pound gymnast, one of the youngest and smallest in the history of the Olympic Games, scored the first perfect 10 (on bars) and warmed the hearts of millions. Before the close of the Games, Nadia had scored a total of seven perfect scores. Nadia won the Olympic all-around title as well as the balance beam and uneven bars events. She earned a silver medal in the team event and a bronze medal on floor exercise.

Actually, the only problem Nadia faced was dealing with the media at press conferences following the competitions. She was shy and very seldom smiled or showed expression. She only managed to say that she was pleased with her results and was not surprised by scoring the first 10 in international competition, because she had scored plenty of others in previous competitions.

Never before in Olympic history, in the years of thousands of routines, had a man or woman received a perfect 10. In fact, Nadia's 10 caused many problems for the meet organizers because the electronic scoreboard was unable to accommodate the high score. Instead of flashing a 10, the scoreboard flashed a 1, but there was no doubt as to what the real score was.

Nadia appeared on the covers of *Time, Newsweek,* and *Sports Illustrated* all in the same week! Little girls all over the world, including thousands of American girls, were mimicking her ending pose on floor exercise and hoping they could become the next Nadia.

Nadia Comanici in 1978

World-famous Bela and Martha Karolyi discovered Nadia at age six doing cartwheels better than all of her kindergarten classmates. They gave her a test including interest level, flexibility, style, speed, and competitive nature, and to no one's surprise, she passed with flying colors! The Karolyis invited Nadia to join their hardworking gymnastics school. Nadia had to move away from home to train and live at the gymnastics school. She became the most hardworking, fearless, dedicated little gymnast the Karolyis had ever seen.

After her success at the 1976 Olympic Games, Nadia's life became very good. She was truly a hero in her country. She was invited to all types of parties and social functions and everyone from school kids to state officials wanted to see and talk to Nadia. She and her teammates were given awards never before given to athletes. All the attention was great, but the gymnasts had no time left to train and were losing the desire. They lost their discipline, stamina, size, and technical abilities.

They also lost their great coaches. In a political move, the organization of the Romanian National Team was removed from the Karolyis, so Bela and Martha left to open up a new gymnastics school in Deva.

It was back to the drawing board for the Karolyis. They repeated the same process they had used before when they found Nadia. They visited schools and looked for young girls who showed gymnastics potential. They worked hard with their new, young gymnasts, and the Romanian government invited the Karolyi gymnasts to compete in the Friendship Cup in Cuba. History repeated itself and the Karolyis' gymnasts did very well, winning many medals and awards. They returned to Romania and again won many medals and awards at the Romanian National Championships. In fact, the Karolyis' gymnasts took first through sixth in the all-around at the Romanian National Championships, defeating all the current National Team members. Nadia, however, was not even competing in the National Championships because she was not prepared.

It was after this competition that Nadia approached the Karolyis and asked them to take her back and get her in shape for the upcoming World Championships in 1978. Nadia had gained forty pounds and was very out of shape. Bela told Nadia that she would have to train very hard, get back in shape, learn new routines, and get dedicated once more. Nadia agreed because she wanted to be a champion again. About the same time, the Romanian Federation also approached Bela and asked him to once again be the national coach and take the gymnasts to the 1978 World Championships. With Nadia out of shape and many young and inexperienced gymnasts on the Romanian team, the Karolyis had their work cut out for them. Nonetheless, they worked hard and went to the 1978 World Championships in better shape than they had expected. In fact, the Romanian team earned the silver medal in the team competition and seven individual medals. Nadia, who had lost thirty-five pounds, even won the gold medal on the beam.

Nadia came back at the 1980 Olympic Games in Moscow to win two gold medals on the beam and floor exercise and two silver medals in the team and all-around competition. This was the Olympics that many non-Communist countries (including the United States) boycotted to protest the Soviet Union's invasion of Afghanistan.

Nadia won the all-around at the European Championships in 1975, 1977, and 1979, the only gymnast to win three times. As a three-time winner, she was awarded the European Challenge Cup. In 1984, Nadia was awarded the IOC Olympic Order and in 1993 was inducted into the International Gymnastics Hall of Fame.

It was reported that Nadia was planning to attend the 1984 Olympic Games in Los Angeles, but she announced three weeks prior to the Games that she was retiring from the sport to become a coach and judge.

Nadia defected from Romania to the United States a few years later. She got in touch with an old acquaintance, Bart Conner, with whom she had shared the all-around title at the 1976 American Cup competition in Boston. The two former gymnasts began dating and in 1996 were married, hosting a huge wedding in Romania.

Bart was a member of the 1984 Olympic gold medal team and was the champion on parallel bars. He is the only American gymnast, male or female, to win gold medals at every level of national and international competition. He was a junior national champion, an elite national champion, a Pan American Games champion, a World Cup champion, a World Championships champion, and finally an Olympic champion.

Bart and Nadia spend most of their time on the road traveling and working in the sport of gymnastics. They even own a gymnastics school in Oklahoma.

Mary Lou Retton

The next big superstar in gymnastics was the United States' own Mary Lou Retton. It was mentioned earlier that thousands of little girls hoped to be the next Nadia, and eight-year-old Mary Lou was one of them!

Mary Lou, from Fairmont, West Virginia, was born January 24, 1968, the youngest of five children. She started dance and tumbling class at age four. She vaulted to the head of the class quickly and by age five began taking two gymnastics classes per week. At age seven she transferred to a gym called Aerial-port where she began perfecting her abilities. Finally, on New Year's Day in 1983, just shy of her fifteenth birthday, she packed her bags and her family drove her to Houston, Texas, to train at world-famous Bela Karolyi's gym. (Karolyi and his wife Martha had defected to the United States from Romania in 1981.)

The four-foot, nine-inch powerhouse vaulted into the history books at the 1984 Olympic Games when she scored a 10 on her vault to win the all-around title, the first American to ever accomplish this feat. Mary Lou was inspired by watching her idol, fourteen-year-old Nadia Comanici, at the 1976 Olympic Games. Although Mary Lou looked like perfection during the 1984 Olympic Games, there was doubt a few weeks prior to the Games whether she would even be able to compete at all. Her right knee locked up and she was not able to walk.

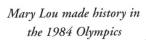

Mary Lou made history in the 1984 Olympics

Her knee did not respond to treatments. She had no choice but to have knee surgery in June 1984, just six weeks before the Games. She took a private jet to Virginia, where one of the best knee surgeons in the country removed cartilage from her knee arthroscopically. Doctors gave her a slim chance to be 100 percent by the Games, but Mary Lou beat the odds. She went through a great deal of rehabilitation and was back to the gym in no time.

Mary Lou was known for her great speed and power. She broke the mold of the so-called typical gymnast look with her stocky and muscular build. She was able to vault and tumble like no one else. She did a double layout salto on floor exercise that was incredible. (A double layout on floor exercise is still a big skill in today's gymnastics, fourteen years later!) She also added a second twist to the already difficult Tsukahara full vault, making it a double twist. Mary Lou also invented a new move on bars called the Retton flip or the Retton salto. She created the skill by accident when one of the elements in her bar routine went wrong and she landed sitting on the bar.

By July, after knee surgery, she was back to full speed and ready to compete. Although many Communist-bloc countries boycotted the Olympic Games, Romania did compete. Romania was where Mary Lou's toughest competition would come. Ironically, her toughest competitor, Ecaterina Szabo, had been trained since she was five by Mary Lou's coach, Bela Karolyi. Sure enough, the competition came down to these two gymnasts.

It all hinged on Mary Lou's last event, the vault. To win the all-around title and become the first American woman to win an Olympic gold medal, Mary Lou needed a perfect 10. A 9.95 would have tied her with Szabo and of course anything less would have meant a lower place in the standings. A vault typically lasts about ten to fifteen seconds, and it was all riding on that one vault.

Mary Lou on the beam

When the green light flashed, Mary Lou was also off like a flash, running with all her might down the runway. She hit the board, blocked off the horse, and stuck her vault. Her arms went up in jubilation and she smiled from ear to ear. *Sports Illustrated* called Mary Lou's vault "A Vault Without Fault." The scoreboard flashed 10 and the crowd went wild. The rest is history!

She said in an interview later that she knew from her takeoff that she had done it. All of her hard work certainly paid off, especially when they put the gold medal around her neck and played the national anthem. She sang the anthem as she watched the American flag being raised in the air.

Mary Lou qualified for all four individual-event finals and earned more medals than any other athlete at the 1984 Games, including silver medals on vault and in the team competition, bronze medals on uneven bars and floor exercise, and the gold medal in the all-around competition.

Mary Lou competed in the 1985 American Cup, winning her third consecutive title. She was the only female gymnast to accomplish this feat, which was her last in the sport of competitive gymnastics. Retton announced her retirement after the 1985 American Cup and went into commentating, motivational speaking, finishing school, and a multitude of other things.

Mary Lou has tried her hand at acting, appearing in the motion pictures *Scrooged* and *Naked Gun 33 ⅓*. She has made appearances on numerous television shows, including *Guiding Light, Knots Landing,* and *Dream On,* and guest-starred in one of the highest-rated episodes of the series *Baywatch.*

Mary Lou has earned countless awards and honors, including the 1984 Sports Illustrated Sportswoman of the Year and 1984 Associated Press Amateur Athlete of the Year; she was the first gymnast and youngest inductee into the USOC Olympic Hall of Fame and the first woman to appear on the Wheaties cereal box; and she is one of America's top ten most admired public figures. In 1994, the U.S. Olympic Committee established the annual Mary Lou Retton Award for athletic excellence. In 1995, First Lady Hillary Rodham Clinton presented Mary Lou Retton with the Flo Hyman Award in recognition of her spirit, dignity, and commitment to excellence. Mary Lou was selected a member of the official White House delegation representing the president at both the 1992 and 1998 Olympic Games.

Mary Lou travels the world as a "fitness ambassador" promoting the benefits of proper nutrition and regular exercise.

Mary Lou married Shannon Kelley, an investment broker, in December of 1990. The couple have two girls: Shayla Rae, who was born in 1995, and McKenna Lane, who was born in 1997. According to Mary Lou, both girls are perfect 10s!

Other Women's Gymnastics Stars

There have been many well-known gymnasts from around the world. Although the ones mentioned above are probably the most popular besides the Magnificent Seven (who we will discuss in a later chapter), there were many other top-notch women gymnasts with great stories.

For example, **Larissa Latynina** of the Soviet Union competed in three Olympic Games. She won the all-around in 1956 and 1960 and earned six medals in her third Olympic appearance in 1964, at the age of twenty-nine and as a mother of two. She was the greatest gymnast in the world in the fifties and early sixties. Larissa won more than twenty-five medals in the Olympic Games, World Championships, and European Championships. She won the all-around at the 1970 and 1974 World Championships. Even after her retirement at the age of thirty-two, she remained active in gymnastics, serving as a coach of the Soviet National Team. In fact, she was the Russian National Coach when Olga Korbut was just fourteen years old. Larissa also served as a member of the Women's FIG Technical Committee.

Czechoslovakia's **Vera Caslavska** won the Olympic all-around titles at the 1964 Olympics Games in Tokyo, Japan, and at the 1968 Olympic Games in Mexico City. She also medaled in all four events at both Olympic Games and won a total of four gold medals in the individual events alone. She was the only female Czechoslovakian gymnast to win a World or Olympic all-around title. She won the 1966 World Championships all-around title and led her country to its only team title. Vera was inducted into the 1991 Women's Sports Foundation Hall of Fame.

Lyudmila Tourischeva of the Soviet Union was dubbed the "Queen of Gymnastics." She was one of only three women to win back-to-back World Championships all-around titles. At sixteen she won her first gold medal at the 1968 Olympic Games, where she and her teammates also earned the team gold. In 1970, she was crowned World Champion. A more mature Tourischeva, although sometimes overshadowed by her young teammate Olga Korbut, claimed the 1972 Olympic all-around title. At the age of twenty-two, she won her second World title. At her last competition, the 1976 Olympic Games, she won another team gold medal, a bronze in the all-around, and a silver on vault.

Cathy Rigby became America's heroine in 1970 when she won the silver medal on the beam at the World Championships, the first female American gymnast to earn a medal at a World Championships. She led the United States team to its best finish in a nonboycotted Olympic Games—fourth at the 1972 Olympic Games. She finished tenth in the all-around. She retired having won twelve international medals. As a tribute, Cathy was honored as one of America's Most Influential Women in Sports on ABC's Wide World of Sports. She went on to have a family and a career as an actress.

The Soviet Union's **Yelena Shushunova** won the Games in 1988, scoring four perfect tens in the process. She edged out Romania's Daniela Silivas by a mere .025. Yelena was a dominant force in the world of gymnastics from 1985 to 1988. At the 1985 World

America's sweetheart,
Cathy Rigby, in 1971

Championships, she won the all-around title and the vault. She finished second behind Aurelia Dobre of Romania at the 1987 World Championships but moved back on top in 1988 to win the all-around gold. Although she didn't capture the same attention as Olga, Nadia, or Mary Lou, she did show the world through her exciting routines that the sport was moving up in its level of difficulty.

Aurelia Dobre became the first Romanian gymnast to win the all-around title at the 1987 World Championships. In fact, her performance spurred Romania on to defeat the powerful team from the Soviet Union. Aurelia earned five medals, including the gold in the team, all-around, and beam events, and bronze medals on floor exercise and vault. In 1988, she came back to Olympic competition. Despite a knee injury, she helped her team earn the silver medal.

Another Romanian star, **Daniela Silivas,** won the silver medal in the all-around at the 1988 Olympic Games in Seoul, South Korea. She also won gold medals on the beam, bars, and floor exercise and the silver team medal at the 1989 World Championships.

Phoebe Mills, a former speed skater who held an international age-group record for the 500 meters in speed skating, became the first American female gymnast to win an individual event medal at an Olympic Games when she won the bronze medal on the beam at the 1988 Olympic Games. An interesting note is that when Phoebe retired from gymnastics and left coach Bela Karolyi, she moved on to a new and exciting sport—diving. Phoebe successfully competed in diving while at college.

Brandy Johnson was ranked the highest American all-around gymnast among men or women at the 1988 Olympic Games with her tenth-place finish. Brandy's finish equaled the 1972 finish of Cathy Rigby. Brandy earned a silver medal on vault at the 1989 World Championships and finished seventh all-around. Her final competition was the World Cup in 1990, where she placed fifth all-around.

Svetlana Boguinskaia is a three-time Olympian from Russia, competing in the 1988 Olympics at age fifteen, the 1992 Olympics at age nineteen, and the 1996 Olympics at age twenty-three. She won four medals at the 1988 Olympic Games, including the gold on vault and in the team competition, the bronze medal in the all-around, and the silver on floor exercise. Her longtime coach Lyubov Miromanova committed suicide only three days after the 1988 Olympic Games. Many speculated that she was depressed with Svetlana's bronze-medal finish in the all-around, among other things that were happening in her life. Svetlana said later, "When I lost her, I lost the thing most dear to me in my life." Svetlana took the news very hard and stopped training, saying that she couldn't make herself go to the gym. Fortunately, after a few weeks, Svetlana went back to the gym and began training with a new coach. In her first two major events after her coach's death, Svetlana won the all-around title at both the 1989

Svetlana Boguinskaia

World Championships and the 1989 European Championships.

Svetlana, nicknamed the "Belarussian Swan" for her beauty and grace, won every event at the 1990 European Championships, scoring 10s on floor exercise and the balance beam. At the 1990 Goodwill Games, she was the all-around silver medalist. At the 1992 and 1996 Olympics, Svetlana was the captain of her team and earned the gold medal in the team competition in Barcelona, Spain.

America's own **Kim Zmeskal,** from Houston, Texas, shocked the world in 1991, winning the all-around title at the World Championships on her home turf of Indianapolis, Indiana. Kim, who was coached by Bela Karolyi, became the first American, male or female, to win the World Championships title—and she beat Svetlana Boguinskaia doing it.

Kim and Svetlana were fierce competitors at the 1991 World Championships, taking first and second, respectively, in the all-around. However, in 1992, Svetlana moved to the United States and began training with Kim at Karolyi's Gymnastics. The two became good friends!

Kim Zmeskal trained at Karolyi's Gymnastics since she was very small, and Mary Lou Retton was her idol. Karolyi would tell Mary Lou Retton to look at her "little sister" when Kim would tumble. Bela used to affectionately call Kim his "little bitty bug" and "the hope—my next great gymnast."

Many skeptics, including Svetlana, claimed that the only reason Kim won the World Championships was because she was on her home turf. Kim came back strong at the 1992 Individual Event World Championships to win the balance beam and floor exercise titles, proving that she was the pre-Olympic favorite for the all-around title.

Although Kim was expected to win a medal in the all-around at the 1992 Olympic Games in Barcelona, she took a devastating fall off the balance beam in the compulsory round of competition and finished tenth all-around. However, she still helped her team earn the bronze medal.

Kim Zmeskal

The Soviet Union's **Tatiana Gutsu,** known for the tremendous amount of difficulty in her routines, earned the all-around title at the 1992 Olympic Games, just barely edging out (by a toepoint) the United States' Shannon Miller. Gutsu also won the 1992 European Championships and took fifth at the 1991 World Championships.

Because of her gymnastics success, Tatiana was awarded a three-bedroom apartment for her and her family in 1992. Prior to this, Tatiana and her mother, father, older sister, and two younger sisters lived in a two-room dwelling in Odessa.

In 1996, the Olympic title was won by eighteen-year-old **Lilia Podkopayeva** from Ukraine. Lilia, who started the sport at age seven, displayed grace and difficulty in all her routines from her head to her toes. She's probably best known for her outstanding tumbling on floor exercise, complete with an Arabian double front salto with a half twist. Lilia dedicated her Olympic all-around title to her grandmother, who died while Lilia was on her way to the Olympic Games in Atlanta. Lilia's grandmother traveled with her to training six days a week while Lilia was growing up. Lilia knew her grandmother would want her to compete at the Olympic Games. Lilia was thrilled to be able to dedicate the win to her greatest fan! Lilia also won the European Championships in 1996. She went on tour in the United States with the American team and learned to speak English very well. The American women's team became great friends with Lilia.

The 2000 Olympic Games are fast approaching and the world awaits the next superstar in the world of gymnastics.

Chapter 7

The Magnificent Seven

The nickname "Magnificent Seven" refers to the 1996 U.S. women's Olympic gymnastics team. The term was coined for marketing purposes at the pre-Olympic exhibition in North Carolina just weeks before the team won its first-ever Olympic gold medal for U.S. women's gymnastics. The Magnificent Seven team included Amanda Borden, Amy Chow, Dominique Dawes, Shannon Miller, Dominique Moceanu, Jaycie Phelps, and Kerri Strug.

Amanda Borden

Amanda Borden was born May 10, 1977. She is from Cincinnati, Ohio, and trained at Cincinnati Gymnastics Academy with her coach, Mary Lee Tracy. (Tracy was selected as the 1996 women's Olympic team assistant coach.)

Amanda, nicknamed "the Pepsodent Kid" because of her beautiful smile, started gymnastics when she was seven, and six years later made the 1990 National Team. It was obvious early on that she was talented. In fact, at the 1991 World Championships, she was selected to demonstrate the new 1996 compulsory routines.

Amanda suffered great disappointment in 1992 when she took seventh all-around at the Olympic Trials, just missing a spot on the

Olympic team that traveled to Barcelona, Spain, and won the bronze team medal. However, instead of quitting the sport, she persevered and remained on the Senior Women's National Team for the next four years. In fact, she was among the top four in the country from 1993 to 1996.

Amanda went on to make three World Championships teams, one in 1993 and two in 1994. At the 1994 Individual Event World Championships in Brisbane, Australia, Amanda qualified for the uneven bar finals and earned eighth place. At the 1994 Team World Championships in Dortmund, Germany, Amanda helped her team earn the silver medal.

The "Pepsodent Kid"

Amanda won two gold medals in the all-around and team competition, and two silver medals in the all-around and floor exercise events, at the 1995 Pan American Games in Mar del Plata, Argentina.

When the 1996 Olympic Trials came around, Amanda took fifth all-around, securing a spot on the Olympic team. She was made captain of the 1996 Olympic gold medal team. She is known as the

"Winning the gold medal proves to me that hard work pays off!" said Amanda Borden. When asked what it was like to see her face on the cover of the Wheaties cereal box, Amanda said, "It's weird, but neat!"

Amanda has skills on the balance beam named after her in the FIG *Code of Points*. One skill is a side-split jump (split greater than 180 degrees) with a half turn. Another is a straddle pike jump with half turn (split greater than 180 degrees) in side position.

encouraging, motivating, and optimistic one. She always has a kind word and a smile for everyone.

One of the first years that Amanda made the National Team, she attended a National Team meeting. After the meeting, Amanda went up to the gentleman representing an apparel sponsor of USA Gymnastics and thanked him and his company for supplying her with leotards, warm-ups, shoes, and other items. This truly summarizes Amanda. She's always polite and appreciative and eager to help others. Her outgoing personality and genuine love of the sport made her a favorite with the media during the highly publicized Olympics.

Amanda was offered a gymnastics scholarship to the University of Georgia prior to the Games, but after earning the gold medal at the Olympics, she decided to turn to professional gymnastics competitions, shows, tours, and exhibitions. She would have liked to do both collegiate and professional competitions, but there is an NCAA rule that states you cannot earn money from competitions and still maintain your collegiate eligibility. She—and all her teammates—

were faced with a tough decision. They all decided to accept money and forego their college gymnastics careers.

Although Amanda retired from international gymnastics competitions after the 1996 Olympic Games, she still competes in professional events like the Reese's International Gymnastics Cup, the Rock 'N Roll Event, Professional Championships, and other fun and entertaining events. She also travels the country doing gymnastics tours and attends a college in Ohio.

Amy Chow

Amy Chow was born May 15, 1978, in San Jose, California, where she still lives. She trained at West Valley Gymnastics with coaches Mark Young and Diane Amos.

Amy began the sport when she was three years old. Her mother wanted Amy to be a ballerina, but the dance school wouldn't enroll Amy at such a young age—so instead she started gymnastics.

Amy was always the quiet, shy member of the Magnificent Seven. Many thought she was just shy around those whom she didn't know well, but her coaches said that she was also quiet during gymnastics practice.

Amy may have been quiet, but she sure had a lot going on in her head. She has many talents and is a shining star in whatever she tries. She excelled not only in gymnastics but also at playing the piano and in her schoolwork. Amy is an accomplished pianist, and has taken piano lessons since 1982. She received the advanced level certificate of merit from 1993 to 1996, and also played in the National Piano Auditions for fourteen years. Amy also competed in diving during the summers as she was growing up.

As for school, Amy attended a college preparatory all-girls school throughout high school and maintained a 4.0 grade-point average.

This is tough enough to do in itself, let alone training long hours at the gym and traveling around the world competing! Amy has competed in Puerto Rico, France, Argentina, Germany, Japan, and Mexico, not to mention nearly everywhere in the United States, in her gymnastics career.

Fortunately, she stuck with gymnastics because she went on to do great things in the sport. She became a member of two World Championships teams. In 1994, she helped her team earn the silver medal at the Team World Championships in Dortmund, Germany. In 1996, she was a semifinalist on vault at the Individual Event World Championships in San Juan, Puerto Rico, and finished fifteenth in this event. She qualified to compete in the 1995 World Championships in Sabae, Japan, but sprained her ankle two days prior to her departure and could not make the trip. She won gold medals in the team event and on

Amy Chow at the 1996 Olympics

vault, a silver medal on parallel bars, and a bronze medal in the all-around at the 1995 Pan American Games in Mar del Plata, Argentina.

Amy is known as a great twister and bar worker. She competed a beautiful triple full twist on the floor, a standing full twist on the beam, and a double twisting double back flyaway dismount on bars. She even has two skills named after her on the uneven bars.

She was a great asset to the Americans during the 1996 Olympics. She not only earned the team gold medal, becoming the first Asian-American gymnast to medal, but she also earned the silver medal on uneven bars.

After earning her Olympic medals, she decided to forego the gymnastics scholarship she was offered to Stanford University. Like Amanda, she now competes in professional competitions and travels the country doing tours and exhibitions. She is attending Stanford University as a student, not as a gymnast. She hopes to one day become a pediatrician.

"Winning the gold medal at the Olympics means that I've accomplished my dream," said Amy Chow. And the best part of winning the Olympic gold medal? "My own satisfaction and feeling of pride."

In Amy's first semester at Stanford, she had to take her name tag off her dorm-room door, because she was receiving so many visits from her fellow students!

Dominique Dawes

Dominique was born November 20, 1976, in Silver Spring, Maryland. She is affectionately known as "Awesome Dawesome" to her teammates and friends, a nickname that has stuck with her fans and the media. Dominique trained at Hill's Angels in Gaithersburg, Maryland, and was coached by the gymnastics club's owner, Kelli Hill. Dominique started gymnastics when she was seven years old.

Even when she was young, Dominique was very powerful and explosive. In fact, she invented a tumbling pass one day at the gym, thanks to her powerful legs. The floor exercise mat was just a little short of the standard forty foot by forty foot mat, so, for safety purposes, Coach Hill put an additional mat at one end of the floor so the gymnasts would not tumble off the larger mat. Coach Hill told the gymnasts that if they hit the mat at the end of the floor exercise, they had to immediately tumble back in the other direction. Dominique hit the mat

"Awesome Dawsome"

nearly every time she tumbled, so she got very good at tumbling one way and then immediately tumbling back the other way. This is how she developed the "up and back" pass that she is known for. She performed eleven skills all linked together in one tumbling pass!

Hill coached Dominique her entire career and saw her potential from the beginning. Dominique even lived with the Hill family for a few months prior to the 1992 Olympic Games in order to train more hours and alleviate distractions outside the gym.

Dominique was a National Team member from 1991 to 1997. She was a member of both the 1992 Olympic bronze medal team and the 1996 Olympic gold medal team. She also won the bronze medal on floor exercise at the 1996 Olympic Games in Atlanta. Dominique was the oldest member of the 1996 Olympic team, and became the first African-American woman to medal in the sport of gymnastics. (Jair Lynch also medaled at the same Olympic Games, becoming the first African-American male to medal in the sport.)

Dominique was a member of five World Championships teams. She won

Dominique Dawes said, "The Olympic gold medal has meant so much to me, but even without it, I would still be proud and satisfied with my Olympic Games experience."

two silver medals, on uneven bars and balance beam, at the 1993 World Championships in Birmingham, England. She also finished fourth all-around at this event, just missing an all-around medal. At the 1994 Individual Event and All-Around World Championships, she was once again headed for an all-around medal—but a slip on vault dropped her to fifth in the standings. She helped her team win the silver medal at the 1994 Team World Championships in Germany, and won the bronze medal on the beam at the 1996 World Championships in Puerto Rico.

Her biography includes three pages of events in which she has competed, including gymnastics competitions in Puerto Rico, Japan, Germany, Australia, Great Britain, Spain, France, and the Netherlands. Some countries she's visited more than once!

Dominique had a very distinguished gymnastics career. In addition to the outstanding accomplishments listed above, she won the 1996 Olympic Trials and all four individual events at the 1996 National Championships. She also swept the all-around and all four events at the 1994 National Championships, making her the first gymnast to accomplish the feat since Joyce Tanac Schroeder won the all-around and all four events at the 1969 AAU National Championships.

Since the 1996 Olympics, Dominique has retired from international-level competition but is still competing in professional competitions and doing tours and exhibitions. She is also pursuing other interests, and has appeared in the Broadway hit *Grease* and in the Artist Formerly Known as Prince's music video "Betcha By Golly Wow." She's also trying her hand at modeling and acting.

Shannon Miller

Shannon Miller was born March 10, 1977, in Rolla, Missouri, but grew up in Edmond, Oklahoma. She is the most decorated American gymnast, winning more World and Olympic medals than any other

American gymnast—male or female—in history!

How did it all begin for Shannon? Her parents bought her a trampoline and enrolled her in a gymnastics class at age five. In 1986, Shannon's club traveled to Russia for a clinic. Shannon saw some of the best gymnasts in the world and tried to duplicate their skills. She cried in frustration and worked hard to try and keep up. Coach Steve Nunno was also in Russia and was impressed by Shannon's abilities. He invited her to

Shannon Miller

train in his club and within two years Shannon was competing at the national level. Two years later she was considered world class and won her first international medal at the 1990 Catania Cup in Italy.

Shannon, unlike some of the gymnasts on the National Team, was able to live with her mom, dad, sister, and brother, and attend normal public school while she trained. She even graduated on time with her senior class! Shannon attributes most of her success to having a solid support system within her family. She maintained a 4.0 grade-point average while training and competing all over the world. Shannon was also active in several charities including the Oklahoma Red Ribbon Campaign for Drug Free Youth, Pediatric Aids fundraiser, and Children's Miracle Network Telethon. She also donated money, food, and time to help victims of the Oklahoma City Murrah Federal Building bombing and participated in a television special to help children cope with the disaster. Another project of Shannon's was holding the "Shannon Miller Silent Auction" to raise funds for a teacher at her high school with leukemia. These are just a few of the many contributions Shannon has made to her community. Shannon has always said that she feels it is important to give back to the sport that has given her so much.

In terms of gymnastics competitions, she contributed there, too! She made her first World Championships team in 1991 and helped her team win the silver medal—the first team medal of any kind for the United States at a World Championships. She also became the first American woman to qualify in all four individual events and tied for second on uneven bars.

Two months before the 1992 National Championships, Shannon dislocated her elbow and had to have surgery in which the doctor inserted a microscrew in order to repair it. She missed only one day of gymnastics practice and was back in the gym conditioning and doing as much as she could. She attended the National Championships and was leading the compulsory round of competition. She and her coach decided to scratch from the optional round of competition, which meant that making the Olympic team was riding on her sole performance at the 1992 Olympic Trials. All the other gymnasts used part of their score from the National Championships and part of their score from the Olympic Trials. Shannon performed beautifully at the Trials, making the team with ease.

At the 1992 Olympic Games in Barcelona, Shannon just missed winning the all-around gold medal by a toepoint. Instead, the fifteen-year-old settled for the silver in the all-around behind the Unified Team's Tatiana Gutsu. She also won a silver medal on the balance beam, helped her team to earn the bronze medal, and won bronze medals on the uneven bars and floor exercise.

Shannon's five medals at the 1992 Games were the most Olympic medals won by an American athlete in any sport.

At the 1993 World Championships, Shannon won the all-around title, becoming only the second American gymnast to accomplish such a feat (Kim Zmeskal was first in 1991).

She contemplated quitting after the 1993 World Championships because her back was hurting and she felt she had accomplished all there was to accomplish. She talked it over with her parents, who said they were behind her 100 percent, but they also suggested she discuss it with her coach, Steve Nunno. After meeting with Steve, Shannon discovered that she was feeling bored because she didn't have any

When asked what winning the gold medal has meant to the sport of gymnastics in the United States, Shannon Miller said, "It means a great deal because it showed we can accomplish anything with teamwork!"

goals. So, she and Steve set some new goals—like competing in the Goodwill Games, winning two World Championships all-around titles, and possibly competing in the 1996 Olympic Games.

Setting goals certainly helped, because she continued her winning streak at the 1994 World Championships, becoming the first American gymnast to win back-to-back titles. Internationally, only three female gymnasts had accomplished this feat prior to Shannon's performance in 1994.

She won the 1995 Pan American Games and helped her team earn the gold medal as well. Although the slightly injured gymnast didn't earn an individual medal at the 1995 World Championships in Sabae, Japan, she did help her team earn the bronze medal.

Shannon won the 1996 National Championships but could not participate in the 1996 Olympic Trials due to an injury. She petitioned onto the Olympic team and, under the direction of head coach Martha Karolyi, helped her team earn the historic gold medal in Atlanta. As icing on the cake, Shannon also won the gold medal on her favorite event, the balance beam! She showed poise and maturity on all the events and proved to the world that she and her teammates were the best.

Shannon won a total of seven Olympic medals and nine World Championships medals from 1991 to 1996. She's a three-time Sullivan Award nominee (1993, 1994, and 1995), an award honoring the top amateur athlete in the U.S.A. She's won the Dial Award, Zaharias Award, Master of Sport Award, Sports Headliner of the Year Award, Henry P. Iba Citizen Athlete Award, and three-time USOC SportsWoman of the Month Award, just to name a few.

Shannon retired from competitive gymnastics in 1997 but, like her teammates, still competes in professional competitions, tours, and exhibitions. She also attends school at the University of Oklahoma, where she studies math and physics. She would like to attend graduate school once she has earned her degree. She tried her hand at acting when she played herself on the television series *Saved by the Bell.* She had a great time and hopes to pursue acting, motivational speaking, and commentating for gymnastics on

Edmond—Home of Shannon Miller

Interstate 35, which runs through Edmond, Oklahoma, between Memorial and Danforth, was renamed the Shannon Miller Parkway on April 9, 1998. Also, the Liberty Park in Edmond, Shannon's hometown, was renamed the Shannon Miller Park. In addition, the city of Edmond is planning to erect a $100,000 eighteen-and-a-half-foot-tall bronzed statue of Olympic gold medalist Miller that will be placed in the park to honor this star gymnast for all of her accomplishments!

television. She also wrote a book about her life in the sport, entitled *Winning Every Day.*

Dominique Moceanu

Dominique Moceanu was born September 30, 1981, in Hollywood, California. She and her family moved to Illinois and then Florida before finally settling in Houston, Texas, so that she could train at Karolyi's Gymnastics. She trained with Bela and Martha Karolyi for five years leading up to the 1996 Olympic Games.

Dominique's parents are from Romania. Her father was a member of the Romanian Junior National Team and her mother was a gymnast in Romania, too. Her parents defected from Romania in 1980 to move to America. Dominique's father, Dumitru, had always dreamed of his

Dominique Moceanu

child being a gymnast. When he was growing up, Dumitru's mother had forced him to quit the sport to focus on education. Dumitru and Camelia, Dominique's mother, made a commitment before Dominique was even born to give their child the opportunities Dumitru was denied. When Dominique was only three years old, Dumitru put her up to a clothesline and let her hang to test her grip. As you might expect, she was very strong! This is when Dumitru phoned Bela Karolyi for advice about his young daughter. Karolyi told him, "Be patient." So Dumitru followed this advice and waited until 1991 to make his move to Houston and Karolyi's Gymnastics.

Dominique, who resembles Nadia Comanici, is known for accomplishing great things at a young age. She first made the USA Junior National Team at age ten, the youngest gymnast ever to make the team. She became Junior National Champion at age twelve.

The very next year Dominique won the Senior National Title at age thirteen, the youngest recorded champion in the history of American gymnastics.

Future Champion

After Dominique won the Junior National Championships at age twelve, she began signing autographs, "Dominique Moceanu, 1996 Olympic Champion, for sure."

"The best part of winning the team gold medal in Atlanta was the feeling of pride for my country," says Dominique.

She's also the youngest gymnast ever to have an autobiographical book published on her life, which only included thirteen years at the time.

At age fourteen, Dominique was the youngest member of the 1996 Olympic team! The minimum age to compete in the Olympics in 1996 was fifteen. Since Dominique would turn fifteen in 1996, she was eligible to compete. The FIG changed the age minimum from fifteen to sixteen but, fortunately for Dominique, it took place in 1997, the year after the Games.

And it was fortunate for the American team that Dominique could compete in the 1996 Olympic Games because she helped her team earn the gold medal. She also took ninth in the all-around competition, fourth on floor exercise, and sixth on the beam.

Prior to the Games, Dominique earned the only individual medal for the United States, a silver on the beam at the 1995 World Championships in Sabae, Japan, and was the highest American all-around finisher.

She earned her first international title at the 1995 Visa Challenge and became the United States Olympic Committee's Athlete of the Month for April and September 1995. She was a nominee for the 1995 Sullivan Award, which honors the most outstanding American amateur athlete.

Dominique's enormous popularity has paid off! She was featured on the cover of *Vanity Fair* magazine in 1996 and appeared in a Kodak television commercial. She even models a local clothing line in Houston. Her book is entitled *Dominique Moceanu: An American Champion.* Dominique even has her very own gym—she and her family opened a gym called Moceanu Gymnastics in Spring, Texas, in 1997.

Dominique was the only member of the Magnificent Seven to continue training for international competition after the 1996 Olympics.

It was tough to continue to train with all the professional competitions she entered, the tours, and the appearances that filled her schedule (not to mention school, to which she had returned on a full-time basis). Her life was hectic but nonetheless she competed in the 1997 John Hancock U.S. Gymnastics Championships and finished ninth in the all-around, third on vault, and second on floor exercise. Because some of the top six gymnasts were not age-eligible to compete at the World Championships, Dominique made the World Championships Team and traveled to Lausanne, Switzerland, for the 1997 World Championships. Despite the hurdles of having an inexperienced team and a difficult draw (the Americans had to compete in the first of eight subdivisions, and usually the scores rise, so it's best to be in the last subdivision), the Americans finished sixth and Dominique ended up fourteenth in the all-around.

World-famous Bela Karolyi has coached not only Dominique,
but Olympic champions Nadia Comanici, Svetlana Boguinskaia, and Mary Lou Retton!

Dominique's bubbly personality shines through whenever she competes. Her exuberance and excitement have made her a favorite with her fans.

Dominique brings fans out in record numbers. Judging by the amount of mail she receives at the USA Gymnastics office, she may be the most popular gymnast today! Many fans would like to see her compete at the 2000 Olympic Games, but Dominique says that she's taking it one day at a time.

Jaycie Phelps

Jaycie was born September 26, 1979, in Indianapolis, Indiana. She lists Greenfield, Indiana, as her hometown and began the sport of gymnastics at age four when her nursery school teacher suggested she try it.

Jaycie made a huge jump in the sport between 1993 and 1994. At

the 1993 National Championships, she finished twenty-fourth all-around in the junior division. By the 1994 National Championships, she finished sixth all-around in the senior division. At that competition, she not only made her first National Team but she also earned the right to compete in the World Trials competition. She finished fifth all-around at

Jaycie Phelps

the World Trials and was on her way to Dortmund, Germany, to compete in the 1994 World Championships. As the youngest member of the World team at age fifteen, Jaycie still competed like a veteran! She was a big factor in the United States' silver medal finish. (It's interesting to note that six of the seven members of the 1996 Olympic team were members of the 1994 World Championships Team.) Although there was no all-around award given at this competition, Jaycie finished fifteenth at the conclusion of the optional finals. Jaycie also had a vault named after her at this competition, being the first in the world to perform it.

Jaycie credits most of her success to her coach, Mary Lee Tracy, and Cincinnati Gymnastics Academy, where she trained with teammate Amanda Borden.

Jaycie continued climbing the gymnastics ladder when she finished third all-around at the 1995 National Championships. In the 1996 National Championships, Jaycie was second after compulsories, just behind Shannon Miller, and came back in optionals to lead the first three rounds of competition. However, Shannon pulled ahead

"Winning the gold medal at the Olympic Games has made all the long days in the gym and the ups and downs worth it," said Jaycie Phelps.

on her last event—bars—scoring a 9.85 to win the title over Jaycie, 78.38 to 78.33.

Jaycie finished third in the Olympic Trials and was off to Atlanta, where she helped her team earn their first-ever gold medal! Jaycie finished seventeenth in the all-around in the team competition but could not advance to the all-around finals because only three gymnasts per country are allowed in the finals.

Following the Games, Jaycie went on a tour and did many professional competitions, but she was having a lot of trouble with her knee. Finally, at the end of 1997, Jaycie had knee surgery to repair the damage. The actual surgery involved transplanting a meniscus cartilage from a donor into Jaycie's knee. The doctor gives athletes undergoing this surgery a fifty-fifty chance of competing again at the highest level. Over the course of a year, Jaycie's own tissue will actually replace the transplanted structure. It's the success of this healing process that will determine whether Jaycie will have the opportunity to compete again.

As for her future, she's just going to take it slow and see how things go. We hope to see Jaycie back in action and preparing for the upcoming World Championships and Olympic Games.

Kerri Strug

Kerri was born November 19, 1977, in Tucson, Arizona. She is the youngest of three children, all of whom were involved in the sport of gymnastics. Her father is a heart surgeon and her mother works in the home.

Kerri first made the USA National Team in 1991 and competed in the 1991 World Championships, helping her team earn the silver medal.

Kerri was the youngest member of the 1992 Olympic team in Barcelona that earned the bronze medal. Although Kerri finished fourteenth all-around, she was unable to advance to the all-around finals because three of her teammates were ahead of her in the standings, and the rules allow only three gymnasts per country to enter the finals.

Kerri was a member of the 1993 World Championships Team and took fifth all-around, fifth on vault, and sixth on floor exercise. At the 1994 Team World Championships, Kerri helped her team win the silver medal. At the 1995 World Championships, she helped her team earn the bronze medal. Kerri represented the United States in five World Championships events and two Olympic Games. She was a seasoned, steady performer and her teammates and coaches relied on her to bring in solid scores.

Although Kerri experienced a great deal of success in her career, many times she was frustrated by playing second fiddle to gymnastics greats such as Kim Zmeskal, Shannon Miller, and Dominique Moceanu. However, she was very talented in the sport—and earned many titles to prove it, such as the 1993 World Championships Trials, the 1995 U.S. Olympic Festival, and the 1996 McDonald's

Nadia-crazy!

Kerri had a favorite movie while growing up, *Nadia*, which was the story of Nadia Comanici's life and her 1976 Olympic experience! Nadia was one of Kerri's gymnastics idols. In fact, at Kerri's eighth birthday party she invited about ten of her friends to her house and put on her favorite video. She thought it would be her best birthday party ever! After only about ten minutes into the movie, several of her friends had gone outside to play. By the end of the movie, only Kerri and one friend were left. Kerri was crushed that her friends didn't understand her love for gymnastics!

American Cup title, defeating 1992 Olympians Svetlana Boguinskaia from Belarus and Oksana Chusovitina from Uzbekistan.

At her last major competition, the 1996 Olympic Games, Kerri received the attention of the entire country and gained celebrity-status for her courageous vault. Kerri is probably one of the most popular of the Magnificent Seven because of her vault on an injured ankle that many assumed clinched the gold medal for the United States' team.

Here's the scenario: The U.S. team had a small lead over Russia after three events. The U.S. team was on vault and the Russian team was on floor exercise. Dominique Moceanu, who was the next-to-last vaulter for the United States, missed both vaults. The pressure was intense for eighteen-year-old Kerri, who was the last vaulter. Kerri, who was always so solid on this event, missed her first vault and injured her ankle. She limped back to the runway and her teammates and coaches cheered her on. During the second attempt she landed the vault but then fell to the ground clutching her ankle in agony. The Georgia Dome crowd went wild, cheering for the American team, who now had a little breathing room under the intense pressure of the strong Russian team. However, everyone was concerned by Kerri's injury, which turned out

Kerri made history at the 1996 Olympics

The Magnificent Seven

to be torn ligaments in her ankle.

Actually, the U.S. team did not need Kerri's vault to win the gold, but at the time it appeared that way because Russia was still competing on floor exercise.

The image of Kerri being scooped up in the arms of her coach, Bela Karolyi, and being carried to the award stand to receive her gold medal along with her six teammates will be one Americans will not soon forget.

Kerri showed a great deal of determination and courage as she went 100 percent for the second vault despite her injury. She said later at a press conference, "I've trained all my life for this moment and I wasn't going to risk losing the gold medal for an ankle injury."

Although Kerri made the all-around finals and event finals, she was unable to compete due to her ankle injury. But she was heralded as a hero for her courageous performance at the 1996 Olympic Games and even earned the Olympic Spirit Award, which was presented by Carl Lewis at a press conference after the Olympic Games.

Kerri was featured as one of the ten most fascinating people in 1996 on a Barbara Walters special, and she appeared on the popular televi-sion series *Touched by an Angel* and *Beverly Hills 90210*. She was also invited to many prestigious social functions, including President

"Winning the team gold medal was an accomplishment of a lifetime goal and the fulfillment of a dream," said Kerri Strug.

Clinton's fiftieth birthday party. Kerri was able to meet stars like Tom Hanks, singer/actress Brandi, tennis star Andre Agassi, and the cast of the television show *Beverly Hills 90210,* just to name a few.

Kerri is studying communications at UCLA and is a volunteer assistant coach for her school's women's gymnastics team. She joined the Kappa Alpha Theta sorority and is a spokesperson for the Children's Miracle Network and Special Olympics. Like her teammates, she participates in tours, exhibitions, and professional competitions, and makes special public appearances. She also wrote a children's book on her life entitled *Heart of Gold.*

CHAPTER 8

RESOURCES

Organizations

USA Gymnastics
Pan American Plaza
201 South Capitol Avenue
Suite 300
Indianapolis, IN 46225
(317) 237-5050
Fax: (317) 237-5069

United States Olympic Committee
One Olympic Plaza
Colorado Springs, CO 80909
(719) 578-4529
Fax: (719) 578-4677

International Gymnastics Federation
Rue des Oeuches 10, Case postale 359
2740 Moutier 1
Switzerland
41 32 494 64 10
Fax: 41 32 494 64 19

International Olympic Committee
Chateau de Vidy
C.P. 356
1007 Lausanne
Switzerland
(41 21) 621 61 11
Fax: (41 21) 621 62 16

NCAA
6201 College Boulevard
Overland Park, KS 66211-2422
(913) 339-1906
Fax: (913) 339-0026

Note: The NCAA is relocating to Indianapolis, Indiana, in the summer of 1999.

Amateur Athletic Union
P.O. Box 10,000
Lake Buena Vista, FL 32830-1000
(407) 934-7200
Fax: (407) 934-7242

Magazines

There are three magazines dedicated exclusively to gymnastics that are published in the United States. One is *USA Gymnastics,* which covers primarily American gymnastics competitions and athletes, as well as major competitions leading up to and including the Olympic Games. Another publication is called *Technique,* which is geared toward the coach, judge, or administrator of the sport. For subscription information regarding *USA Gymnastics* or *Technique,* call 1-800-345-4719.

The other publication is *International Gymnast*. This magazine covers American as well as international competitions and athletes. For subscription information call (405) 447-9988.

Books

Bohnert, Craig. *USA Gymnastics Media Guide.* Indianapolis: USA Gymnastics, 1998.

Cohen, Joel. *Superstars of Women's Gymnastics.* New York: Chelsea House Publishers, 1997.

Feeney, Rik. *Gymnastics: A Guide for Parents and Athletes.* Indianapolis: Masters Press, 1992.

Karolyi, Bela and Nancy Richardson. *Feel No Fear.* New York: Hyperion, 1994.

Lessa, Christina. *Gymnastics Balancing Acts.* New York: Universe, 1997.

Marks, Marjorie. *A Basic Guide to Gymnastics: An Official U.S. Olympic Committee Sports Series.* Glendale: Griffin Publishing, 1998.

Miller, Shannon and Nancy Richardson. *Winning Every Day.* New York: Bantam Books, 1998.

Schenk, Brian. *The History of USA Gymnastics: The Early Years Through 1991.* Indianapolis: USA Gymnastics, 1997.

Seeley, Jan Colarusso. *Rookie Coaches' Gymnastics Guide.* Champaign: Human Kinetics Publishers, 1992.

Strug, Kerri and John P. Lopez. *Landing on My Feet: A Diary of Dreams*. Kansas City: Andrews McMeel Publishing, 1997.

Whitlock, Steve. *Make the Team: Gymnastics for Girls*. Boston: The Time Inc. Magazine Company, 1991.

USA Gymnastics Safety Handbook. Indianapolis: USA Gymnastics, 1998.

GLOSSARY

Aerial – The gymnast does a cartwheel in the air without touching her hands to the ground.

Amplitude – Gaining height on gymnastics skills such as a leap or a release move on bars; the degree of execution of a movement. In general, the higher the skill or the more breathtaking the movement, the better the amplitude and the score.

Arch – The upper and lower portions of the back are stretched backward in a curve, like the shape of a banana.

Borden – There are two Bordens on beam, named after Amanda. The first skill is a side-split jump (split greater than 180 degrees) with a half turn. The other is a straddle pike jump with half turn (split greater than 180 degrees) in side position.

Bridge – An arched position with hands and feet flat on the floor and the stomach raised.

Chow – The Chow on bars is a stalder backward to handstand on high bar with a one-and-a-half turn after handstand phase to mixed-L or L grip. This skill is named after Amy.

Dawes – Dominique has a skill named after her on the bars. It's a handstand on the high bar, followed by a giant circle backward to handstand with one-and-a-half turn in handstand phase.

Dismount – The last move off the apparatus at the end of the routine or the last tumbling pass on floor exercise.

Flip-Flop – Starting from a standing position, the gymnast jumps backward to land on hands, then pushes off hands to land back on feet (sometimes called a back handspring or flic flac). This skill usually comes before big tricks in tumbling passes on floor exercise. It's also used a lot on the balance beam.

Giant Swing – A swing on the uneven bars in which the body is fully extended and moving through a 360-degree rotation around the bar. The men also do giant swings on both parallel bars and the horizontal bar.

Handstand – Hands are flat on the floor shoulder-width apart, legs are together, and the body is completely extended and in a vertical position. This is a basic element and, once mastered, can be used on vault, uneven bars, balance beam, and floor exercise.

Hollow – The stomach and upper chest are rounded forward in a curve.

Layout – The body is straight and completely extended.

Miller – The Miller on bars is a cast handstand with one-and-a-half turn after handstand phase to mixed-L or L grip. This skill is named after Shannon.

Mount – The first move that gets the gymnast onto the apparatus or the first tumbling pass on the floor exercise.

Phelps – The Phelps on vault is a half turn on the horse, followed by a half turn into a stretched salto forward off the horse. This vault is named after Jaycie Phelps.

Pike – A position in which the legs are straight and the body is folded at the waist.

Quadrennium – A period of four years from one Olympic Games to the next.

Release Move – Leaving the bar to perform a move before regrasping the bar.

Routine – A combination of elements displaying a full range of skills on one apparatus. Routines are either compulsory (all the gymnasts perform the same routine), or optional (the routines are individually choreographed).

Salto – The gymnast starts from a standing position and rotates 360 degrees in the air to land back on the feet. Basically, a salto is a flip in the air. Sometimes the skill is referred to as a front flip or back flip. It differs from the flip-flop in that you don't use your hands.

Straddle – A position in which the legs are straight and apart.

Strug – The Strug on floor, named after Kerri, is a tour jeté with additional half turn (180-degree split) to land on both legs.

Tkatchev – A giant circle backward to a backward straddle release over the bar to a hang on the bar.

Tuck – A position in which the knees and hips are bent and drawn into the chest. The body is folded at the waist.

Yurchenko – A vault that is preceded by a round-off onto the board, a flip-flop onto the horse, and a back one-and-a-half salto off the horse.

INDEX

U.S. $7.95
Can $10.95

Whether you're a budding gymnast or simply a die-hard fan, if you love gymnastics, this book is for you! Explore the exciting world of the summer Olympics' most popular sport with this comprehensive, entertaining guide. *The Gymnastics Almanac* includes information ranging from superstars such as the Magnificent Seven to competitions to finding your own coach. Also included are resources such as Web sites, national and international associations, organizations, and clubs devoted to gymnastics.

Luan Peszek is the Publications Director at USA Gymnastics, the sport's national governing body. She is also a gymnastics coach and a former gymnast.

Includes dozens of photos, sidebars, and safety tips!

A ROXBURY PARK BOOK

LOWELL HOUSE JUVENILE

LOS ANGELES

NTC/Contemporary Publishing Group

7 46623 00795 7

ISBN 1-56565-966-X

50795>

9 781565 659667

W7-BJB-353